Adoption and Fostering

A PRACTICAL GUIDE

ALISON KING

The Crowood Press

First published in 1989 by
The Crowood Press
Ramsbury, Marlborough,
Wiltshire SN8 2HE

British Library Cataloguing in Publication Data

King, Alison, 1950–
    Adoption and fostering: a practical guide
    1. Great Britain. Children. Adoption & foster care
    I. Title
    362.7'33'0941

ISBN 1 85223 133 5

Acknowledgements

Many thanks to those couples who agreed to be inter-
viewed for the purposes of this book: Mr and Mrs Killey,
Mr and Mrs Thomas and Mr and Mrs Rollins. Thanks
also to the colleagues and friends who have read the
manuscript, and whose comments have been invaluable.

Dedication

For Laura and Charlie.

Typeset by Consort Art Graphics   Exeter   Devon
Printed and bound in Great Britain by Biddles Ltd,
Guildford & Kings Lynn

Contents

Many books about social work refer to the social worker as 'she' and the child as 'he'. Sometimes I have stuck with this convention, but I have also called the social worker 'he' or 'he or she'; the child has also been 'she' or 'he or she'. I hope this rather random use of gender, done in an attempt to avoid sexism, isn't too irritating!

There will be some words and phrases used in this book that are not generally familiar, or are used in a particular and unfamiliar context. Rather than explain the precise meaning of each every time it is used, I have added a glossary of these at the end of the text.

This book concerns itself with the law and social work practice in England and Wales; Scottish readers may find much of the information useful but should bear in mind that the law relating to children and families is different in many respects in Scotland.

Foreword

The last twenty years or so have seen many changes in relation to adoption and fostering. In 1966, 22,792 adoption orders were made in England and Wales; by 1986 the total figure had dropped to 7,892. Developments have tended to reflect wider changes in society, and the reduced availability of babies for adoption arising from improved methods of contraception, the introduction of legal abortion, and greater acceptance and support for single parents.

Recent years have brought exciting new initiatives in finding families for children who would at one time have been regarded as not 'fit for adoption'. Recognition of the need for permanence and security has also fuelled the emphasis on family placement for most children entering care – both for short periods and for those children unlikely to be able to return to their family of origin. A major shift has occurred in attitudes towards trans-racial placements – typically arrangements for black children to be cared for within white families. Now most agencies recognise that where a child cannot remain with his or her own family, then every effort must be made to recruit a family of the same race and culture.

All this should be set within the context of supportive work with birth families. Research published in 1973 provided startling evidence that if a pre-school or primary school age child remained in care for as long as six months, the chances of a return home were slim. Subsequent work confirms this pattern. Here is strong evidence of the need for effective services to prevent reception into care and, when this is unavoidable, intensive work aimed at improving family functioning so that the child may return home as quickly as possible. It is here that there is an important role for the foster carer who will need training and support in this vital work with the child's family.

There is a move, albeit slow, towards developing a more equal partnership between social workers and substitute parents. Too often the emphasis has been on assessment, rather than on a mutual exploration of needs and expectations which can lead to better informed and more realistic decision-making.

This book is a welcome contribution to the information available for those contemplating caring for someone else's child and should also provide a useful source of reference for those already experienced in this demanding but rewarding work.

Pauline Bibby
Director
British Agencies for Adoption and Fostering

Introduction

Most people probably look after someone else's child at some time or other. Perhaps you have a grandchild to stay, take care of a neighbour's child while she does the shopping, or entertain your daughter's schoolfriend for tea. In all these situations you take on the immediate responsibility for that child; if she falls over and breaks her leg, her mother would think you very irresponsible if you did not get medical help, for example. However, her parents are still the most important adults in her life, and they make all the decisions, big and little, that affect her everyday world.

Children who can't live with their own parents have to be looked after by someone else, and these days this usually means living with another family. They could live in children's homes with many other children, and be looked after by skilled and dedicated members of staff who, none the less, go on and off duty and are not around for twenty-four hours a day. Sometimes this will be the right place for a child, but for most children the best place is a family – not a 'perfect' family, but just an ordinary group of people living together (or maybe one person living alone), who can give the child the experience of day-to-day life as someone who belongs. After all, when children grow up, they will probably have families of their own to look after; how can they do this properly if they haven't had any practice at family life as children? If you're reading this book, you probably agree with this point of view; as you read on I hope you will get an idea of what it's like to care for other people's children as adoptive or foster parents.

In Great Britain there are about 90,000 children 'in care' at any one time. This means that their parents can't look after them, and the local authority's social

7

services department has taken on some of the parental responsibilities until the children can go back home to their own families. The majority of these children are white, but many do come from minority cultures, such as the Afro-Caribbean and Asian communities. There are also significant numbers of children in care who have parents of different races. At present the proportion of 'black' (to use the general term to include children from all these groups) children in care is not matched by a similar proportion of black foster and adoptive parents. Social workers are keen to recruit more black families, since most people believe that the best place for a child is with a family from a similar culture.

Many people think of fostering and adoption as simply 'looking after other people's children'. To begin with, the two are very different from each other – more detail about the exact differences will be given throughout the book, but, put simply, fostering is a way of caring for children on a temporary basis until their permanent future homes can be decided upon, whilst adoption involves the taking on of all the rights and responsibilities of a legal parent for a particular child. People who plan to adopt often foster the child for a while first.

In fact, having someone else's child to live with you, whether for days, weeks, months or years, is a very complicated and sometimes confusing business. Many foster parents say 'we treat them just like one of our own', meaning that if one child gets a packet of sweets so does the other one. If their child goes on a school holiday they will do their best to see that the foster child can go too, and both children get the same number of cuddles and stories at bedtime. That's wonderful, and many foster parents perform near miracles to try to make the 'other' child feel part of the family, but for all sorts of reasons he or she never will, and never should, be 'just like' one of their own children.

If you adopt a child, then he or she will become a permanent member of your family, and will be, legally, your own child. Even then, none of the family will ever forget that he or she is adopted, or that another family gave the child life. These memories of the child's 'birth' family are important for the child and the adopting family, as we shall see in more detail later, and an adopted child will never be quite the same as children born to you, the adopting parent.

Children will remain a very important part of their own families, even while they are not living with them. Their parents won't forget them, and many children will have clear memories of their mums and dads. 'Substitute' parents (a term used to cover people who foster and adopt) will never completely take the place of 'birth' parents (often also called 'natural' parents). Natural grandparents and brothers and sisters can sometimes be very much a part of the fostered (and sometimes adopted) child's life too, and arrangements will often be made for such relatives to keep in touch through visits or by phone or letter. Lastly, when children are not living with their parents, there is usually a social worker involved who will be in touch with all the family and the child on a regular basis.

The history of fostering goes back several hundred years, and right up until the nineteenth century 'boarding out', as it was called, was seen as a way of 'rescuing' children from feckless parents who could not look after them. In those days, the families who took in these children were very much left to get on with caring for the children with hardly any supervision from any authority, and very little in the way of financial help. In other words, fostering was seen as a charitable act, and the foster child was expected to show gratitude for this, probably by working on the land or in the house.

In many of these situations the children remained permanently with their foster families, but adoption did not become possible in law until the twentieth century. Various acts of parliament made it permissible for a non-relative lawfully to become a child's parent, and the most important of these were passed in 1958 (Adoption Act) and 1975 (Children Act). For further information on the law concerning fostering and adoption, *see* Chapter 6.

There are many children in Britain today who need new families to live with. Their ages range from 0 to 18 and their personal histories are as varied as are the children themselves. Fortunately, there are also many families who want to help these children by giving them a home, but sometimes the two don't match. Families coming forward who want to foster or adopt can be disappointed to discover that the child they had pictured as needing them does not exist. Perhaps this book will help to give people thinking about taking on the care of someone else's child a realistic idea of what to expect, both from the children themselves and from those involved with them.

Finally, one important message will be repeated throughout the book – looking after other people's children is hard, demanding (emotionally and physically), full-time (24 hours a day, not 9 to 5!), voluntary work. Foster parents have many skills, and are expected to perform many different tasks: your patience and good humour must be endless, and for all this you are (usually) paid only expenses sufficient to feed and clothe the child. As adopters, you too will be in for a period of hard work whilst the child settles into your family, but you have a different goal from foster parents. You will want the child to put down good, strong, healthy roots in your family and you will be prepared to work hard at getting to know the child, and helping him or her to come to regard you as mum and dad, in order to achieve this. All hard work has its rewards, and for substitute parents there is no greater pleasure than seeing an unhappy child relax and start to smile again within their family.

1   The Children

There is a whole variety of reasons why children can't live with their own parents, ranging from those which are very straightforward to those which are very worrying and hard to understand. Most children in the middle of a family crisis will be looked after by relatives, or will stay with one or other parent, and will never need to be taken into care or be looked after by strangers. People still think that many of the children who need looking after are orphans; this is not usually so, as, again, relatives will take the child in after the death of the parents.

Social workers talk about children 'coming into care', 'being received' or 'taken into care'. This means that the local authority where the child lives will take over some of the responsibilities of a parent for that child, a social worker will become involved with the family, and the child will go to live somewhere away from home. Sometimes, parents themselves ask for their children to spend some time in care, and sometimes it is the authority which decides that the children would be at risk if they stayed with their parents, and makes the decision for the children to live elsewhere. For more information about the technicalities of the 'care system', *see* Chapter 6.

DIFFERENT CHILDREN WITH DIFFERENT NEEDS

A Simple Situation?

Imagine a single mother, a long way from her own parents, living alone with her 3-year-old daughter. She is rushed to hospital in the middle of the night with acute appendicitis – what will happen to the little girl? If there are no relatives or friends who can help, the night duty social worker is called, and contacts foster parents who have agreed that they will be available to take children in an emergency during the night. The little girl is taken to their house. Arrangements are made for the child to visit her mother regularly while she is in hospital, and when she comes out the mother is delighted to have her daughter back home again. From the social worker's point of view this is a very simple situation, in which the mother needed purely practical help to tide her over a difficult time.

However, the most simple situations have a habit of becoming complicated when human beings are involved. Think again about the example above, and imagine the following. The mother comes out of hospital and seems to be reluctant to have her daughter home; she says she doesn't feel well enough, she's short of money and her flat is damp. The social worker talks to her about these difficulties, and the mother admits that she is worn out by the responsibilities of being a single parent, and doesn't think she can cope for much longer. She loves her daughter, but is frightened she might lose her temper one day and hit the child. So it seems that the girl will need to stay with her foster parents a little longer while her mother and the social worker look at ways of making her feel better about her life and her role as a parent.

This will not be an easy job for the mother or for the social worker, but the likely outcome is that the little girl will return home before too long. Sometimes, however, mothers in this situation come to the conclusion (usually after many weeks or months) that they can never properly bear the responsibilities of being a parent. In this case, social workers would seek a family to look after the child permanently – to adopt her. This example has been taken to the extreme in order to demonstrate that seemingly 'easy' situations can have far from easy solutions. However, it must not be forgotten that the vast majority of children who come into care do go back to their own

12

families within a very short space of time (about six weeks), so in all probability our family were happily reunited!

Sarah

'You see, the trouble is, her dad – well he isn't her real dad, *he* went off when she was only a baby – he favours the two lads, well they're his, aren't they, it's only natural.'

All families have problems and difficulties to overcome, and for families where the children are not all the natural children of both partners, as in the quote above, these can be all the more trying. The children of most stepfamilies do not come into care, but of the children who are in care a high proportion come from families where dad is not really dad. Sarah, whose mum is quoted above, is 10, and her two half-brothers are 3 and 4. Sarah's stepfather expects her to help a lot in the house, and thinks she should do more than most people would ask of a child of this age. Sarah has been looking very sad at school; she's got no friends, she always wears scruffy clothes and sometimes she smells. She doesn't talk about her family – she doesn't talk about anything much. Although she's not doing at all well at school her teacher thinks she's actually quite clever – she arranges for special tests which show that Sarah is indeed a bright child who could be doing a lot better. One day Sarah finally confides in her teacher that she is frightened of her stepfather, who she says hits her, and she doesn't want to go home. Because of all these worries about Sarah, the social worker who knows the family makes the difficult decision to take her away from her mother and stepfather and give her some time in a foster home. In this situation Sarah's mother agrees reluctantly that her daughter should spend some time in care. If she hadn't agreed it is still possible that the decision to remove Sarah from home could have been taken, but without her mother's consent.

Darren

Foster parents are usually asked to take children straight from their own homes – as in the two examples above. Children who go to prospective adoptive parents, on the other hand, will almost never be taken to live with them direct from their own homes, but will previously have been living either in children's homes or in foster homes. An adoptive mother describes how this baby came to live with her and her husband:

'Darren had been living with his foster parents since he was four months old; he was eight months when he came to us, and we eventually adopted him when he was just over two years old. His parents weren't in agreement with the adoption, and we found the strain of waiting to see what the judge would decide was very difficult, as we took him on knowing we wanted to adopt him. Now he's ours, it all seems worth while.'

Darren had spent the first four months of his life with his parents, but sadly they were not good at coping with the demands of a small child, and he became ill, needing to go into hospital. Darren's mum was mentally handicapped, and although she didn't mean to hurt or neglect the child in any way, she easily got muddled about feeds, didn't keep him very clean, and used to leave him wet and crying in his pram for long periods. She was given a lot of help; she spent four days a week at a family centre where trained nursery nurses taught her the skills of mothering, but still the baby became ill through her unwitting neglect. The social workers had to put the baby's welfare first, and took him into care against his parents' wishes. Because they believed that Darren's parents would never be able to look after him properly, plans were made for him to go to an adoptive family, whilst he first spent four months with his foster parents. As Darren's new mother said, he was over two by the time they actually adopted him. The judge had agreed with the social workers that, although his parents could give him love, that was not enough to ensure a secure and happy childhood for him.

AT HOME – OR INTO CARE?

Social workers do not like having to take children away from their parents. Our society is geared towards the 'nuclear' family – mum, dad and the kids – and the natural and obvious place for children to grow up is within this family. We should all think very carefully indeed before disturbing this status quo, as sadly some children can have experiences in care that are more upsetting and cause them more problems than what was happening at home. Teenagers who have been in care for long periods have told research workers that, as bad as home was, being in care was much worse. This does not mean that the people who looked after them, whether in foster homes or children's homes, didn't do their very best to make them happy. What it probably does mean, however, is that the love that children have for their parents is so great that things have to be very, very bad indeed before living with strangers is preferable to living at home.

However, society also has a duty to protect its children. Social workers, who take on this duty, have the difficult job of deciding when the risk to children in their own homes is greater than the risk of taking them away. We often talk about what is best for children, but sometimes it can be helpful to talk about what is *least bad* for them – social workers call this the 'least detrimental alternative'. This helps us acknowledge the fact that living away from home is not good for any child, but it may be less bad than living in a situation where violence is an everyday part of life. Perhaps this sounds rather pessimistic, but it is so important not to become complacent about children who are separated from their parents. Social workers, and others in the child care field, must try to think in this way.

Back to Sarah

Admitting a child to care can be a very tempting alternative for the social worker who has to keep an eye on a child like Sarah. She knows that a foster home would be a lovely, clean and comfortable place where Sarah wouldn't have to do the housework and would be able to concentrate on her school work, and she also knows that if Sarah was in a foster home she wouldn't have the constant nagging worry about whether she was safe or not. But weighed up against this is Sarah's love for her mother, her brothers, and probably even her stepfather, who she has known since she was a baby. Sarah is in danger of losing her roots if she leaves home, and we all know that if a young plant has its roots damaged it can be very hard to help it to grow strong and healthy again.

In Sarah's case, however, the risks of staying at home did outweigh the risks of leaving, and she has been much happier since she has been in a foster home, with her school work improving tremendously. So everyone can sit back and congratulate themselves on a good decision, can't they? Most certainly not! The hardest work begins *after* the child has come into care. Think about it – what is the future for Sarah? Her love for, or attachment to, her mother, stepfather and brothers has not diminished since she was taken away from them, but she has become fond of her foster parents and the other children in that home. She feels terribly confused; life is easier and more comfortable in the foster home, but she couldn't possibly admit that to anyone because it would be so disloyal to her mum. She loves to see her mum, which she does once a week, but the meetings are a bit awkward because neither seems to know quite what to say. She went home for the day last week, and she was rather upset to find that one of her brothers had moved into her bedroom. Now she's worried about where she would sleep if she ever did go home, but she daren't ask anyone about this. After all, her mum might – just *might* – say that she wasn't ever coming home and that would be too much to bear. Sarah's whole world has been turned on its head, and she needs a lot of help to understand what's happening and why.

16

Sarah's family need help too. They have to sort out why Sarah is being treated differently from the other children and look at how this can be changed, but at the moment they are still so hurt and angry about what's happened that they can only talk about Sarah changing *her* behaviour to fit in with *them*. They say that Sarah was cheeky and disobedient, and did what she liked in the house, and that this is why she went into care. Anyone who knows Sarah finds it impossible to believe that this timid child, who has few words but a ready smile, and who is so eager to help, could be described in this way.

The social worker wants above all to see Sarah happily and safely returned to her family, because she knows that to become a happy and healthy adult Sarah must be sure and confident that she has a family of her own who love her. She also knows that the longer Sarah stays in care the less likely it is that she will return home. It would be wrong to put Sarah back into the same situation as the one she left, so things must change before a return home is seriously planned. This example illustrates one of the biggest dilemmas in child care – the need to help parents change their attitudes towards a child (which can be a long and difficult, sometimes impossible, process), set against the need to get that child back home before the attachments between her and her parents are too badly damaged.

The role of Sarah's foster parents hasn't been mentioned because this example has simply been an attempt to give a picture of the child's position and the complexities surrounding it. At this stage it is enough to say that, if you were Sarah's foster parents, you would be part of the team all working together to achieve the best for Sarah. Your main contact would be the social worker who would keep you up to date with any developments. You would also attend meetings to discuss Sarah and what should happen to her. Most important, of course, would be your day-to-day contact with Sarah herself, and it would not be surprising if you became her confidant and trusted friend

17

to whom she could talk about things that confuse and worry her. Your role here would be crucial, not only in terms of reacting to Sarah herself in a way that made her feel it was all right to talk like this, but also in feeding back the information to the social worker (with Sarah's agreement), in order to help make the best plans. Future chapters will concentrate in more detail on the vital work the foster parents actually do with the children they look after, and with the parents of these children.

When There's No Future at Home

At the point we have left her, Sarah is very definitely a foster child and the plans are that she should return to her own family. Still, her social workers can already see that there are pitfalls in this plan. Will her parents be able to change their attitudes towards her? Will Sarah want to go home, or will she lose her roots completely? The decision to cut a child off from her parents is very serious, and is never taken without the most careful thought, but if Sarah's parents are unable to provide a home that is secure, safe and loving enough for her, then the social workers must look for new parents who can give her just that.

If a return home doesn't look possible in the near future, it is sometimes tempting to 'wait and see'. Sarah's parents might eventually realise that they must treat their daughter differently, so couldn't Sarah just stay in her foster home for another year or so to see what happens in the family? She could, yes, but her confusion and uncertainty would grow. All the time she has been in care she has become fonder and fonder of the foster parents, but they and the social worker have always told her that she won't be staying there very long. Her mum doesn't always visit when she says she will, and Sarah has stopped missing her little brothers and her stepfather, although she feels guilty about this. She's effectively torn between her birth family and the family she lives with, and she will need a lot of help if she is to 'let go' of her birth family and move on to a new permanent family.

If you were Sarah's foster parents in this situation you would probably also have your own feelings of confusion, particularly if you had become fond of the child. You might find yourself becoming quite angry with her parents if they didn't seem to be doing their best to create a situation where Sarah could go home. It can be very difficult not to pass these feelings on to the child, even if you take care (as of course you would) not to say anything unpleasant about her parents in front of her.

The longer Sarah stays where she is, the worse all these uncertainties become. So, once the child care team who have responsibility for Sarah (and that includes her foster parents) have made the decision that her parents are not going to be able to have her back home in the reasonably near future, a new family who want to make a lasting commitment to her must be found. Several social services departments these days believe that no child should be in care for more than two years. In other words, within that time the child should either be back home or with an adoptive family. This actually helps social workers in their work with the natural parents, as the time limit encourages honesty about what's wrong in the family and a concentrated attempt to help put this right. This is much healthier than the 'wait and see' policy.

'DIFFICULT' BEHAVIOUR AND HOW TO HELP

Attachment

Children in care who are no longer babies have personalities of their own, as well as likes and dislikes, loyalties to their parents, and memories, both pleasant and unpleasant, of what has happened in their lives. Foster parents often have to handle the immediate effects of the upset-

19

ting business of leaving home, and children can behave in a variety of disconcerting ways. An important factor in a child's behaviour when he is separated from his parents is the strength of the attachment between parents and child. The word 'attachment' has been used before, and it describes everything that slowly and gradually binds together the mother or father and their child as they live together through the childhood years. Toddlers hate it when their mum leaves the room without them, and this is a very clear demonstration of 'attachment behaviour', or the need to be close to the person who is most important. Fear increases attachment behaviour, so that a small child will run past a big dog to get to his mother, rather than remain safely distant from the dog, but far away from mother. Although children who have been frequently hit by their parents may be frightened of them, if they are also attached to those parents their attachment overcomes the fear. What this means in practice is that the social worker who goes to 'rescue' the child from the parent who has been hitting him, finds that child clinging to the parent, terrified of being taken away. Social workers are more worried about children who leave their parents to go with strangers *without* a backward glance, because this could mean that the attachment between parent and child is weak or, indeed, non-existent. If there is no strong attachment, something has gone badly wrong in the parent-child relationship which may be very difficult to put right. One example is mothers and babies who are premature, who may not become strongly attached because they have not spent those vital first few weeks in constant contact.

When children of any age who are well and strongly attached to their parents go to foster parents, they will suffer a period of distress and even mourning, particularly if they do not see their parents quickly and frequently. Perhaps they will cry a lot, not eat or sleep properly, and seem to want to have nothing to do with you. This can be very upsetting for foster parents, and puzzling as well if you know that the home from which the children have come is an unhappy and uncomfortable place. Actually, you should be more worried by the children who walk through your front door and seem to settle in happily straight away. These are the children who probably have severe problems in their relationships with their parents, and this may mean that a return home will be difficult to achieve.

Understanding

Children in care will behave in all sorts of ways that you will find hard to understand and to tolerate. We can all put up with a certain amount of bad behaviour, particularly if we understand the reason for it, and there's no doubt that foster and adoptive parents need more than their fair share of tolerance. However, everyone also has their limits, and if the children do that one particular maddening thing too many times, patience may be stretched to breaking point. Many substitute parents say, for example that they find lying very difficult to handle, whilst stealing, rudeness and bullying of their own children are all aspects of behaviour that are fairly common and very upsetting. Perhaps this particular type of behaviour is so difficult to cope with because it seems to be aimed so directly at the foster parent, when all they are doing is trying to help the child settle in their home. However, a foster parent has to realise that children in this situation will not be feeling grateful to them, but instead will probably be very hurt and angry about what's happened, confused about why it's happened and even worried that it might all, in some way, be their fault. If, on top of all this, they don't trust anybody enough to talk to them about these feelings, then their world must be a pretty miserable place and some difficult behaviour is, perhaps, not that surprising. Even adults are not always very good about saying what might be troubling them, so we can't expect children who have been separated from the people they trust to sit down and talk sensibly about their worries.

One lad sticks in my mind as an example of a child who

can't share his feelings. Many years ago I used to visit Micky in his foster home. He'd been there about six months, and before that he had spent a couple of years in a children's home. It was his birthday, and his foster mum had laid out a special tea as a surprise. When he came in from school, she said 'Go and make a cup of tea, Micky', expecting him to react with pleasure to the spread. She was so disappointed when he just came back into the living room and sat down without a word! Micky's emotions were so confused that he simply didn't know how to respond to such a gesture.

Irritating Behaviour

It probably isn't very helpful to list many different types of behaviour that children in care can display, since the child you look after will almost certainly do something that isn't on the list! However, before you make your application to become a foster or adoptive parent, it's very important to think carefully about the sort of things that really do irritate you to distraction. Presumably most of us would be bothered to some extent by persistent lying or stealing, but if you can admit to yourself that you get very unhappy about untidiness, for example, then you may have to come to the conclusion that another child's toys and clothes strewn about would increase your irritation to too great an extent. Alternatively, if you are in the process of discussing the possibility of taking a specific child with the social worker, there will be plenty of opportunity to talk about what the child is like – how he behaves generally, and how he reacts when he's unhappy or upset. It's very important to remember that substitute parents cannot possibly warm to every child who needs a home, and there's absolutely no shame in saying that you just don't think the child under discussion would fit into your family. Inevitably you will have a twinge of guilt at saying 'no', particularly if you pick up from the social worker that she's desperate to find a home for this child.

However, you shouldn't be swayed. Remember that if you agree, perhaps against your better judgement, to take a child, and things later go wrong in such a way that the child has to leave your home, the hurt both to that child and to your family is immeasurably greater than the inconvenience of your having said 'no' in the first place.

Helping

The way in which children behave is influenced by their surroundings and the people they are with, as well as by their past experiences. A child who persistently behaves in a way that one family cannot bear may relax in another setting and no longer be driven to 'bad' behaviour. Children can also be helped to change their behaviour. In order to do this we have firstly to try to understand what makes the child behave in this way. Usually the problem relates to the time before 'care', and will be to do with the relationships within the birth family, and what happened to lead up to the admission to care.

Young children often have unreal ideas about why they do not live with their own parents – one little girl told me recently that she didn't live with her daddy because 'he's naughty and doesn't buy me any toys'. Often the adults have been reluctant to try to explain to young children the reasons why they are not still at home because these are so complicated and potentially upsetting. Still, we must remember that children will almost always reach their own conclusions about why they're in care (like the little girl above), and sometimes these can be more worrying to the child than the truth. I heard of another small child, for example, who thought he was in care because he had broken a cup. A very common aspect of a young child's thinking is that they are responsible for past events: 'if only I had been a good girl perhaps daddy wouldn't have left us' might be a child's own way of trying to sort out what has happened in her family. So adults do have a responsibility to try to ensure that the children have a clear, if simplified, idea of why they live with someone else's mum and dad rather than their own.

However careful the early explanations are, children in care will almost always feel confused about the fundamental problem — 'why can't mum and dad look after me?' In order to help sort out these questions, the adults involved with the child can help the child compile a 'Life Story Book'. Usually some sort of scrap book, this may include the child's birth certificate, photos, letters, drawings and anything else of significance to the child, and can be used to help the child talk about events in the past that are painful to remember or simply muddled. These sessions will be hard work for the child and the adult involved, who should always be someone well known to the child and liked and trusted by him. It won't be a simple process either, for there will be times when the child just can't handle talking about a particular person or time in his life. It would be impossible to do justice to this aspect of work with children in this book. It is, however, something that substitute parents are often directly involved in and should certainly be dealt with in preparation and training groups (*see* Chapter 3).

So if the child who lives with you is behaving in strange or difficult ways, think carefully about the possible reasons before jumping to conclusions. The problem could lie with the school, and may be dealt with fairly easily, or it could relate to rivalry with one of your own children and be perhaps impossible to resolve within your family. As we have seen, the behaviour could also relate to events that took place long before the child came to live with you which will need to be painstakingly unravelled before the child can 'leave the past behind' and concentrate on the present and future. Finally, never feel that you're on your own with difficult behaviour. Talk it over with the social worker, or (often better still) another substitute parent, who can reassure you that you're not the only person to feel that you're banging your head against a brick wall!

WHAT SORT OF CHILD FOR YOU?

When you first start to think about fostering or adoption as something you and your family would like to do, you will quickly start to picture the sort of child you might look after, and you'll probably be wondering not only what sort of children need homes, but also whether you would have any choice of child.

Babies and Very Young Children

At any one time there are many children who need permanent homes because they will never be able to live with their own parents. Whilst the ages of these children vary from very young to almost adult, the one certainty is that the number of small babies that are available each year for adoption has dropped greatly over the last ten to twenty years. There are various reasons for this, such as greater availability of contraception and abortion, and the fact that a single mother is much more readily accepted in today's society than she was in the 1950's. Those couples who want to adopt a small baby will almost certainly have been through the lengthy and distressing process of finding out why they are unable to have children of their own, and there's no doubt that if you are in this situation you will want to give yourselves time to adjust to biological childlessness before you start making enquiries about adoption. If you do decide to go ahead with an enquiry you will have to resign yourselves to a long wait, as the number of couples who want to adopt babies always outnumbers by many times the number of babies available. Different social services departments deal with enquiries about babies in different ways, so it's worth contacting all the departments within striking distance of your home. Some will have basic restrictions on who is able to apply to adopt a baby, such as an age limit, while the church-based organisations will have other criteria, such as membership of that church or religious sect. Some will operate a waiting list, and may add your name to that after collecting the basic details (for example, where you live, your marital status, ages), and will then contact you when a social worker is ready to visit you to start the assessment process. Other departments may just say that their list is closed, and suggest that you contact them again in, say, twelve months. Assuming that all goes well and you are approved as adopters for a baby, you can count on the waiting time between your first enquiry and the child's arrival being anything from two years upwards.

Adopting a baby seems to be the most straightforward form of looking after someone else's child. You will look like a 'normal' family, no one need know that the child is adopted unless you choose to tell them, and the child comes to you with no memories of times with mum and dad to get in the way of your relationship. But it is this very appearance of 'normality' that can cause niggles within the family. For example, an important part of welcoming the 'natural' child into the family is the endless discussion about who she is and isn't like. This doesn't just go on between grandmothers and aunts, but pervades other situations such as mother and toddler groups: 'Isn't she a little tot! But then look at you – she's never going to be six foot, is she!'. If you're adopting a baby you have to work out quite carefully who you're going to tell and why, and try to imagine if not being able to answer the question 'where does she get her temper from?' is going to worry you.

The other big issue about adopting a baby or very young child is the process of explaining that they are adopted, and giving them some information about their birth family. Most people would probably agree that we all have the right to know who our parents were as well as some information about why they couldn't look after us, if this were the case. In the past, however, many well-meaning adoptive parents did not tell their children the facts about their backgrounds until they were adolescent or even adult, and then those facts were often very sparse. These adopters were worried in case information about the adoption and the birth family would make their child restless and unhappy in his adoptive family. In fact, adopted adults who were only told about their status late in childhood often did feel very shocked at this revelation, which seemed to rock the very foundations of their lives and their relationships. They sometimes became quite obsessed with finding their birth families, about whom they had some very unrealistic fantasies. Nowadays, most child care workers and adoptive parents believe that children should be told about their adoptive status when they are very young – too young, in fact, to understand the meaning of the word adoption fully. There is a variety of simple ways of explaining to a very young child that his mother couldn't look after him, without telling him the whole truth, perhaps, but without departing from the basic facts either. As he grows older and asks questions, more detailed information can be offered. Equally, there are ways of assuring the child that he is a much-loved member of his adoptive family: 'We felt so lucky when the social worker asked if you could come and live with us' might be one way of expressing this. Explaining adoption is a big topic which can't be fully covered here. Discussions with social workers and other adoptive parents will help you decide how to tackle the topic with your own child, and there are various publications on the subject which are very helpful (*see* the list of these at the back of the book).

Older Children

If you think that you would like to welcome an older child into your family, then you will quickly become involved in discussions with the social worker about the age and 'type' of child who might fit in best. Obviously if you have children of your own their ages and personalities will be an important aspect of these discussions. Sometimes older children in need of homes are advertised in various publications, such as *The Guardian*, *Foster Care* (published by the National Foster Care Association), and local papers. British Agencies for Adoption and Fostering also runs an invaluable 'photo-listing' service called 'Be My Parent' (BMP). This is a loose-leaf folder with photographs and pen pictures of many children in need of new permanent homes from all over the country. Most social services departments and child care agencies will have a copy of this book, and it's well worth having a look through to get some idea of the type of children waiting for new families. The children's social workers ask for them to be included in BMP if it's proving difficult to find the right home locally, and it's updated fortnightly, so you can be sure that the children you're looking at are waiting for parents right now.

Parent to Parent Information on Adoption Services, a self-help group of adopters which aims to help others through the process of becoming substitute parents and beyond, as well as promoting the needs of children, also publishes details of children in need of new families in their newsletter sent to members. The more progressive social services departments will constantly be promoting children for whom they are seeking families, and you may also see television programmes featuring particular children in need of new families. Obviously this is a very effective way of reaching a large number of people.

If you are attracted by the details of a particular child, a discussion with the social worker about whether or not that child would fit into your family can be easier than a discussion in a 'vacuum' about children in general. Certainly you will have plenty of opportunity not only to state your own feelings about the type of child you feel best able to look after, but also to discuss the reasoning behind these views and perhaps change or expand them when you have heard more about the needs and demands of the children who are available. Remember, though, that the social worker is looking for the right family for the child first and foremost. Your application may not be treated very enthusiastically if it becomes clear that you are looking for a playmate for your 3-year-old or a tennis partner for your Wimbledon-mad 14-year-old. Such expectations would be quite unfair to any child coming into your family because your firm ideas about what he or she should be like would prevent you genuinely responding to his or her own individual needs.

Children with Special Needs

In general, social workers find that children who are already at secondary school, or who have a specific problem like a handicap, or a very complicated background which has left them feeling isolated, confused and unable to share their feelings, are more difficult to place in the right family than younger children who haven't had so many bad experiences. The consequence of this is that there may be many families in your area who would like to offer a home to a pre-school child with no evidence of handicap, but few, if any, families who feel they could share their lives with a severely handicapped 10-year-old or a 13-year-old who has a reputation for aggressive, difficult behaviour. The implications are obvious – your interest in children in need of new families may be followed up very quickly if you are prepared to be flexible about the age of the child, whereas if you are sure that only a young child would fit in with your existing family, you could find yourself joining a queue. By this I don't mean to suggest that you should compromise in order to 'queue jump', but it is worth remaining open-minded, since honest discussions with the social worker will help you refine your ideas about the 'right' child. I remember standing on the steps of the court with one family and their newly-adopted set of two brothers and a sister, big smiles all round, and reminding them of the phone call they had made to me two years before enquiring about adopting a baby!

Of the many children in care at any one time, a significant number will be disabled or handicapped in some way. The phrases 'mentally handicapped' and 'physically handicapped' can be daunting, especially if you haven't had much to do with either children or adults who have disabilities, but it's important to look beyond the 'label' and try to see the child as an individual, as much in need of care as any other child. Some handicaps are very slight and others have a more profound and lasting effect on the child's abilities, and obviously caring for a child with a severe mental or physical handicap is a very demanding task. Those who take on this task, however, usually say that the rewards of helping this special child to cope will outweigh the problems. If you think that you could offer a home to a child from this special group, your social worker would want to discuss this thoroughly with you during the assessment period. There are also many organisations which specialise in work with people with specific disabilities, and they will send information about a particular condition on request.

Some adoption agencies, whose task it is to find homes for those very special children who can't easily be placed, use a video film of the child to show to families who might be interested in giving him or her a home. This gives the family the opportunity of 'seeing' the child without actually meeting him or her, and in this way they can come to a decision about whether they want to carry on with introductions before the child is personally involved in the process. Many families have found that they have responded in an emotional way to a child who didn't fit their 'blueprint' of the type of child they thought they wanted to look after, and videos enable more families to look at a wider variety of children. Comparison with the phenomenon of love at first sight between adults may sound rather sentimental, but our emotions will inevitably be involved in a response to a child and this should be taken into account. Certainly, more and more social workers are realising that photographs, personalised descriptions, and videos of children are an effective way of engaging adults' interest. Possibly, in the future, videos of substitute families will be available, so that social workers and perhaps the children themselves can make a better and more informed choice about where they should live.

Fostering – What Type of Child?

If your primary interest is in fostering, then the specific type of child you want to look after may be a less important issue. Since all fostering is temporary, and many placements last only a few weeks or months, foster parents are not as worried as adopters about responding emotionally to the child with a view to forming a lasting bond – they know that he or she will shortly be moving on. During the assessment process you and the social worker will certainly have discussions about broad age bands that may or may not be acceptable to you, bearing in mind the ages of your own children, if you have any. Foster parents who have laid down very specific guidelines about the type of child they could look after will not, however, be very useful to a busy social services department which needs to place a wide variety of children quickly and with a minimum of fuss.

Brothers and Sisters

No particular mention has been made so far of groups of brothers and sisters who need to live together, but almost all the children who come into care have brothers and/or sisters, whether or not they live with them. Many foster parents have the space to be able to take more than one child, and would welcome a family group for a temporary period, although the influx of two, three, four or even five children can initially make them feel like a stranger in their own home! It is easy to understand that the familiarity of brothers and sisters around can do much to help a

31

child feel less abandoned, so social workers will try to keep such groups of children together, if at all possible. The prospect of adopting more than one child of the same family is a different matter – not only are the physical and emotional demands on you increased, but you also have to find a way into the network of relationships that already exists between the children themselves in order to understand their individual needs. For example, an older sister can often be very protective towards younger brothers and sisters. Perhaps at home she was expected to look after them, and consequently she may have missed out on some of her own childhood. As her adoptive parents you might have to make sure that she had enough time to play and enjoy life for herself, without making her feel that you were taking her little brother or sister away from her.

Mark and Jeanette took on three children whom they adopted; looking back they wish they'd had more practical advice:

'I used to think – well, I'll do that in the evening. But once they were in bed we were like zombies! Too tired to move! It was useful talking to another adoptive mother who had three – we got a more realistic picture of everyday life than we did from the social worker. Now we've made lists of practical tips to hand on to people who come to talk to us.'

'Three is totally different from two. One of them's always able to run off out of reach, or not have a lap to sit on – three into two parents won't go.'

Same Race Placement

Finally, it's important to look at the issue of the child's racial background. Whilst it goes without saying that in a racially mixed society children in care will come from a whole variety of racial backgrounds, at the present time they are not always cared for by adults of a similar racial background. Perhaps you may take the view that it is the child that matters, not the colour of his skin, and that therefore the racial 'mix' of child and substitute parents is not important. This view has been prevalent in social work until relatively recently (partly, no doubt, because most social workers are white), and in years gone by black babies were placed in large numbers with white families. The only concern was that the family should not be overtly racist and would try to help the child overcome any discrimination on the part of other children or adults. Many of these adoptions have appeared to white observers to be very successful, with the children apparently well integrated into their white communities.

However, as black communities began to claim their clear racial identities, social workers were forced to move away from the image of society as a 'melting pot' in which black and white could live in equality and harmony side by side. Many black people would claim that all white people are to some degree racist, and would also argue that black children, for so long removed from black families and placed with whites, should have the opportunity of growing up within their own culture. If you're black you will know how important it is for black children to identify closely with this culture. A childhood with white adults, however sympathetic they are to blacks, can lead to a situation in which the child thinks of himself as white but is often rejected by white society as well as by his own black community, which may treat him as an outcast. The result is that he is left without any clear 'racial identity', not really knowing who he is or where he comes from. If you're white, perhaps brought up in a particular religion, such as the Church of England, you might like to imagine how you would feel about a child of yours going to live with a family from a totally different culture, who practised a religion that was totally alien to you. Many, many black parents and children have had such an experience when the children have needed to go into care.

All children need to be able to think well and positively about themselves, and for children in care this can be difficult to achieve. Ethnic origin is an important part of identity, and all black people have to struggle to maintain a

33

good self-image in the face of any racism they may encounter. It can be doubly hard for black children in care to feel good about themselves, and it's easy to understand that the task of maintaining a positive racial identity will be simpler if the child lives with people from the same racial background. If these adults feel happy and confident about their own racial background, their children will also learn to be proud of their colour and heritage.

As a result of these considerations, many social workers in the child care field have gradually changed their views on 'trans-racial' placements — placing black children with white families — and now try to find families of the same racial background as the child to foster or adopt. However, most social workers are white, and they are used to assessing white couples for substitute parenting. There have been initial difficulties in adapting the assessment processes in such a way that they become acceptable to the Afro-Caribbean and Asian communities. For example, we all have our own ideas about what is and isn't good parenting, and our culture strongly influences these ideas. White social workers will be influenced by the standards which operate in their own cultures, and this may affect the way they assess black families. Gloria and Desmond are a Jamaican-born foster couple, and Desmond commented, in relation to the assessment:

'We were quite happy to talk about our backgrounds, but a lot of black people would find some of the personal questions difficult — it would get their backs up, particularly coming from a white person. You'd have to have a very sensitive social worker for that part.'

The two major national organisations in the field of fostering and adoption, British Agenices for Adoption and Fostering and the National Foster Care Association, have now made it quite clear that they support the principle of 'same race' placements for all children, for the reasons set out above. Social services departments vary in their policies about the placement of black children, but whatever your own racial origin this is something you will want to be clear about. It's probably safe to say that it is becoming much less likely that white families will be asked to take black children, although there are still in existence many satisfactory trans-racial placements which will certainly not be disturbed simply because policies have changed.

If as a white family you are asked to take a black child, whether because the social worker has been unable to find a black family or because he or she does not believe a same race placement to be essential for this particular child, you, and hopefully the social worker, will be asking yourselves certain questions. What is the racial mix of the area in which you live? Do you have a range of black friends so that the child will be relating to black as well as white adults and children? These are two of the most obvious. Alternatively, you may like to seek the views of other substitute parents in your area, perhaps through the local association, before agreeing to take a child from a different ethnic origin. Foster and adoptive parents, particularly if some of them are black, may have important views on this subject which should be brought to the attention of social workers. If, for example, a local group of substitute parents made it clear that they were in favour of a policy of exclusively same race placements, it may be that this would encourage the social services department to work towards recruiting more black foster and adoptive parents, so that trans-racial placements became unnecessary.

Whatever your views, you need to know that this is one of the most important issues around in the field of substitute family care at the moment. The many black children who are living with white families, and their parents, need support, so that they will not feel that their family life and relationships are no longer seen as acceptable now that current thinking has changed.

Many, many children up and down the country need a new mum, or dad, or both. One, or more, of these children could be right for your family, and you could be right for them. But the actual child may be a surprise – your mental picture of a cheeky 5-year-old lad joining your family for good may turn into a ready-made family of three sisters, or a teenager who only stays a few months, or a physically handicapped baby. Your views may well change as you learn about the children in need of care.

2 Different Situations

It's already been made clear that fostering and adoption are very different ways of looking after other peoples' children, and this chapter will look at the variety of situations that come under the umbrella term 'fostering', custodianship (a sort of half-way house between fostering and adoption), and finally at adoption itself. Whatever the means by which you care for children, you will find it hard, time-consuming work which should be treated as a demanding job in much the same way as many full-time, fully-paid jobs — and it's not one you can leave behind you at 5 o'clock.

'Time-Limited' Fostering

When children who come into care are fostered, this will, in almost every case, be seen by everyone involved as a temporary situation. Most social services departments hold a list of foster parents who have been recruited especially to take children on a 'short-term' basis, often straight from their own homes as the result of some sort of family crisis or problem. Some of these foster families will have an agreement with the social workers that, for perhaps one week in every month or so, they will be ready to be contacted in the night to take in children who have come into care as the result of an emergency (like the little girl in the first example in Chapter 1).

In an ideal world, there would be very few real emergencies. Many situations that could lead to an admission to care in the early hours can be foreseen by the social worker. For example, if the social worker is aware that the marital relationship between a particular couple is at rock bottom, the mum has been threatening to walk out for weeks and the dad doesn't come home every night, she will have a good idea that the children may need a time in care while the parents sort themselves out. In such a situation she might contact a foster family and explain the position to them, asking them to be on stand-by, as it were, to take in the children of this particular family. She would also talk to the family themselves about these arrangements so that they would be aware that their children could be looked after if their own position became intolerable. In this way, everyone could be prepared for the possibility of a reception into care, and the foster parents would already know something about the children and may even have been able to meet them and their parents. If the children did then have to leave their parents this would be less upsetting and difficult for everybody than an unplanned crisis, with the children placed with foster parents who knew nothing about them.

Things don't often seem to happen like this, however, for various reasons. Firstly, most departments don't have enough available foster families to enable one to be tied up, simply waiting to see if they are needed to help out with particular children. The sort of situation described above could go on for some time, with the foster family being unable to take any other children. Secondly, some social workers may feel that they would actually be encouraging parents to use the care system by setting up a 'safety-net' in the form of a foster placement. Rather than providing this as a readily available option, they might think that they should be helping parents to cope within their own family and own home. In fact, of course, the planned foster placement may not in the end be used, because the family will find another way round their difficulties, and the family who does not have the safety-net there may fall apart in such a way that an emergency reception into care becomes essential. We would all agree that removing children from their homes in an emergency is distressing and difficult for everyone, most of all the child. Foster parents who have had children placed in an unplanned way might like to ask the social workers if they think, looking back, that the whole sad business could have been better prepared for.

The facts are, then, that if you want to take on this sort of fostering you will be coping with placements that are hurriedly organised and children who come to you upset and confused. As a short-term foster parent you're unlikely to be bored for long – if you're not coping with the immediate aftermath of a placement, you will be involved in the many tasks associated with the smooth running of the placement itself. You will be acting as a very important member of the team whose focus of interest is the child or children in care. This team will include the family's social worker, his or her senior (often called a team leader), a social worker specialising in fostering, the children's parent or parents, and possibly other members of the family, and often other professionals such as the health visitor, general practitioner and school teacher. Last but not least, the children themselves are very important members of the team, and their views on their future should be sought and listened to carefully. Even very young children may want to express their thoughts about their situation, and the substitute parents and the social worker should help them to do this, either privately before a meeting or directly to the team. Many older children can attend the meetings themselves, and contribute to them. All sorts of discussions will go on between various members of this group at different times, all aimed at sorting out what is best for the children and working towards getting them back home as soon as possible.

Meetings and Discussions

Foster parents spend a lot of time talking to the social workers about all aspects of the children's care – how they're getting on at school, their behaviour in the home, and so on. The social worker will also be ensuring that your information about the children is complete and up-to-date during these discussions. At the beginning of any placement foster parents should be given full details of the child and birth family, including important medical information. This should be written down and will of course be kept safely by the foster parents, since some of the material will be sensitive and confidential. As foster parents you can then make your own contribution to the process of planning for the child, based on your knowledge of the situation.

You will be invited to various meetings about the children during their time with you, usually called either 'case conferences' or 'reviews'. If you're not used to discussions with quite large groups of people these meetings can seem rather daunting, but it's important to remember that you are the people who live with this child twenty-four hours a day, and you therefore have information to contribute that maybe no one else in the meeting is aware of. Social workers and doctors are very good at talking, sometimes in a language that isn't that easy to understand, but you can console yourself with the thought that they might not be very good at dealing with the never-ending demands of *your* foster child. Everyone in this meeting has their own skills and experience, and the right to speak up and be listened to. It is the job of the person chairing the meeting to make sure that everyone's view is heard.

During every short-term placement there will be regular meetings between the fostered children and their parents. Sometimes contact will also be maintained with other members of their family, such as brothers and sisters, or grandparents. When you think about the possibility of becoming a foster parent it's most important that you keep in mind the fact that, although you are looking after a child or children in your own home, your relationship with the parents is almost as important as your relationship with the child. These parents will probably visit their child in your home, and the importance of the success of such visits cannot be over-emphasised. (For more on this, *see* Chapter 4.)

As a short-term foster family, you'll have had discussions during your assessment about practical issues such as bedroom space – how many children could you take at any one time without inconveniencing your own family? We have already seen that children often come into care with brothers or sisters, and it's obviously ideal if they can all be placed together. Many foster parents can handle three or four young children at once, as long as they know that the situation won't last long. From the children's point of view, a camp bed or mattress on the floor is probably better than being parted from brothers and sisters. If the prospect of this sort of organised chaos in your well-ordered home fills you with alarm, then it may be that short-term fostering is not for you! As with any fostering situation you always have the option of saying 'no' to a placement, but if the system is to work effectively it is not possible for all short-term foster families to be choosy about exactly the type of child they are prepared to have. This does not, of course, mean that you would be expected to soldier on regardless of your own family's situation, and time off *is* allowed for illness and holidays, provided such breaks in your availability can be planned for. If you're unlucky enough to have a family member fall seriously ill whilst you're looking after foster children, you will be faced with the difficult choice of struggling on or asking for the foster children to be moved, if only for a temporary period.

'Tasks'

As we have seen, the primary aim after any child comes into care is to get him back home as quickly as possible, and the main work of most short-term placements will be towards this goal. Depending on the child, however, there may also be other 'tasks' involved in any particular placement. For example, Leroy comes to you, aged 9, and the social worker explains that his school attendance has been, to say the least, erratic. Luckily you live fairly near his school, and one aspect of the plan for Leroy is that you will try to get him going to school on a regular basis. This could involve you transporting him to school and handing him over personally to his teacher in the morning, and you will probably also need to spend a good bit of time with Leroy talking about why he started missing school in the first place. It's easy to see that the person on the spot is in the best position to tackle this particular issue. In another situation you might be asked to watch out for particular behaviour that the natural parents have complained about – maybe they find their 3-year-old's tantrums intolerable. If you note down the number of times this child has a tantrum you may be surprised to find that they don't seem to be particularly frequent. You will discuss this with the team, and it may be that you will all conclude that the parents' own behaviour is actually bringing on the tantrums that they find so hard to bear. The plan may then involve you in developing a strategy for 'defusing' the tantrums and teaching this technique to the parents.

Bridging the Gap

Despsite the best-laid plans, every child does not return home. As a foster parent you could have a vital role to play in the interim period, between the decision not to attempt further work towards a return home and a placement with permanent parents who will go on to adopt the child. Children who are told that they won't be living with their parents again have a lot of readjusting to do. They will probably need to grieve for the lost relationship with their parents, and may feel very angry with the people who are looking after them, blaming them (wrongly, of course) for the failure of this relationship. Mention was made in Chapter 1 of the importance of work with children to help them come to terms with their past and present situations, and if your foster child is in this 'in-between world' you will be able to help him or her disentangle the past and look hopefully towards the future. It's important that children sort out most of these muddles before they go to live with the people who are to be their permanent parents. If they go full of angry and hurt feelings they may be unable to form good loving bonds with their new mum and dad, and this could wreck the chances of success for that particular placement.

'RESPITE CARE'

All parents feel at some time that they need a break from their children, but if you are the parent of a severely handicapped child, a regular period without the stress of twenty-four-hour caring for that child can be essential. Foster parents can provide such a break, and a family with a handicapped child can be linked with a particular foster family who can look after their child for regular and frequent periods. It's usually possible for this service to be provided without the need for the child to come into care, but the foster parents would receive the same support, payment, and so on as 'full time' substitute carers. As such a foster parent, you would be able to form a lasting relationship with the child and with the family, and could gain considerable satisfaction from relieving the pressure on the family, and perhaps by doing so preventing the child from having to live in an institution. It may be that this type of fostering will be dealt with by someone other than the social worker who works primarily with adoptive and foster parents, so make it clear if you're interested in looking after children in this way.

FOSTER PARENTS AS ADOPTERS

Foster children are not your own. They are looked after by you as foster parents temporarily whilst their future is sorted out. This fact can't be repeated too often, for it would be very wrong to go into fostering believing that it might, one day, lead to adoption. Quite a few children in foster care will eventually be adopted, but for the great majority this will mean moving on to another family who have been prepared for that particular task. There are, however, always some situations in which it becomes clear to everybody that the fostered child, who now needs adoption, should stay with the foster parents, if they agree.

Clare was only weeks old when she went to live with Carol and Vic as a result of an injury caused by her mother. Clare's mum and dad used to visit regularly, and when everyone was happy that she would be safe she went back home, still only 8 months old. Sadly, her mother still couldn't cope with Clare's demands and again she injured her. Luckily, Clare was able to return to the same foster parents. Carol and Vic believed firmly that Clare should eventually go back home, and they worked hard with her parents, particularly her mum, towards this. Unfortunately things didn't work out, and Clare's mum and dad were unable to show, by the way they treated Clare, that she would be safe with them. Clare stopped seeing her parents completely when she was 2, and Vic and Carol knew that the social workers would be considering adoption as the new plan.

'It had never entered my head that we would be allowed to adopt her – not until we had that meeting here with the social worker and team leader, and they asked if we would consider adopting Clare. So many social workers had told us that fostering is not a back door to adoption, there was no way we were going to forget that – and we really did believe that Clare should go back to her parents, so while they were still visiting that was what we were all working towards. When contact with her parents finished completely, we knew adoption was the best thing, but we thought that she would be moved to another family. When they said would we like to adopt her, I just couldn't believe it – I burst into tears!'

Carol and Vic's conviction that they wouldn't be considered as adopters, together with their strong commitment to getting Clare back home if at all possible, had enabled them to work whole-heartedly with her parents, without letting their obvious affection for the little girl lead them to hope that she might stay with them. They were delighted to be asked to consider adoption, and Clare has been a happily adopted member of their family for some years now. But Carol still says to new foster parents (she's involved in training sessions) that, in general, foster parents won't go on to adopt their foster children, and this is what she believes is best for everyone.

You will, of course, become attached to your foster children, particularly the little ones who quickly become attached to you. Children need to show their affection for an adult and should not be discouraged from forming these bonds. Some foster parents worry that this will prevent the child from being able to move, either back to his parents or to a new family, but in fact the children who are attached to an adult move with less lasting upset than those who have lost so much trust that they can't show affection for anybody. I remember very clearly the look of distress on one foster mother's face as she said of a little boy, who she knew would be going home when the time was right, 'You'll have to move him soon – I'm so frightened of him becoming too attached to me, and I'm starting to keep myself distant from him.' She was rightly worried, but when we talked further it became clear that it was *she* who was becoming very fond of the little boy, and that this was what really worried her. We talked this through, and she saw that she should encourage him to show his affection for her. She kept the little boy until his mum could have him back, and allowed him to be close to her whilst helping him remember his affection for his birth mother, who was a frequent visitor. She helped with the move, and both she and the child were, naturally, upset by the parting. I kept her informed about his progress, and she was pleased to hear that he had settled well at home, and delighted by a visit from him and his mother during the school holidays.

45

Different Situations

Like this foster mother, you may find it hard when children you're fond of move away. It's only by approaching a situation with attitudes like Carol's that you can maintain any sort of neutrality in situations like these. If you see yourselves as doing a specific job of work for a child and his or her parents, you'll be able to work with the plan and gain satisfaction from this. If, on the other hand, you find yourself looking at every short-term foster child and thinking 'I wish he could stay for ever', you will end up causing pain to yourself, harm to the child, and damage to his chances of ever going back home.

TEENAGERS

The fostering of those strange and wondrous creatures known as 'teenagers' has always been regarded as a particularly demanding job. Most people reckon that understanding your own adolescent children is quite trying enough! Such young people need a delicately balanced form of care. They don't want a real, 100 per cent 'mum', who'll fuss about clean clothes and eating a proper breakfast, but on the other hand they do still need nurturing towards a truly independent existence. If you've lived with teenagers you'll recognise this dilemma – all adolescents need to be allowed to find their footing in the big wide world without too much restraint, but they also need a shoulder to cry on, and a guiding hand when that same big wide world threatens to overwhelm them.

Teenagers in care have probably been through all sorts of uncomfortable and troubled times, and they do most desperately need adults who have the patience and tolerance to cope with their various moods and behaviours, particularly if they have been in care for some time and have lost all contact with their own families. These youngsters often have some fairly specific 'problem' which

46

might get in the way of them making their way in the adult world. Some may find it hard to get out of bed in the morning and to maintain an acceptable standard of hygiene, for example, whilst at the other extreme some will be confirmed glue-sniffers in need of intensive help and support. A teenage boy or girl who is prone to violent outbursts of temper will find it hard to make lasting relationships or to hold down a job.

If you should decide that you could offer a home to a teenager – and this sort of fostering definitely isn't for everyone – you would be involved, with the team, in working out ways of tackling his or her particular problems. Time is running out for these youngsters, because strictly speaking 'care' ends on their eighteenth birthday. Some will be lucky enough to be in foster homes where they can stay on a bit longer, and some social services departments have special schemes to enable 18-year-olds to continue to live in some sort of sheltered environment, but for many that awesome big wide world awaits them. Many social services departments now run fostering schemes specifically for teenagers, designed to help sort out the muddles of adolescence and being in care and to prepare them for life on their own in a flat or bedsit. Such placements are usually fairly strictly time-limited, and the teenagers make their own commitment to the placement by agreeing a 'contract' at the outset. This means that they sign a paper stating their particular problems and how they'll work towards solving these. Similar contracts are also agreed and signed by the youngster's parents, the foster parents and the social worker, so that everyone knows what is expected of them. Foster parents get a special allowance for this type of fostering.

'PERMANENT' FOSTERING

Most children who are never going to live with their own parents need the security and permanence of a family who

47

wants to adopt them. But there will always be some children for whom adoption is not the chosen plan, but who still need to know that they can stay permanently with their foster families. Some older children, for example, do not want to make that total psychological break with their birth families by becoming full legal members of their substitute families, even if they have no contact with their mum and dad. Other children may continue to see members of their birth families regularly, and because of this it may not be considered right for them to be adopted. Rarely, the legal situation will be so complex that adoption is almost impossible.

You may come to look after such a child, either through having fostered, or because you have approached the social services wanting to adopt, and have then been attracted by a particular child who needs your long-term commitment without this being legally cemented. People feel differently about these situations – for some the label 'adopted' is not nearly so important as the relationship with the child, whereas for others adoption means for ever and the granting of an adoption order has great importance psychologically. You and the rest of the team do need to be very clear about the plans and the reasons why adoption is not the chosen solution for this child; otherwise, a foster placement may simply be allowed to drift into permanence for want of any other decision being taken.

MONEY

If you think you're going to make any money out of fostering, forget it – you're more likely to end up out of pocket than in funds. Many foster parents are perfectly happy with the present arrangement, whereby most social services departments pay an amount to cover expenses and only top this up with an amount paid as a fee if the child in question has some special difficulty which is extra demanding on time or resources. Some local authorities are now recognising that fostering has become more demanding of time, energy and skill over the past decade or so, and are starting to treat foster parents in a manner more akin to other members of their staff. This will be a very slow process, involving the change of many attitudes entrenched over years of thinking of foster parents as volunteers, who looked after children for 'love' rather than financial reward. In fact, in years gone by anyone who dared express the hope that they might be suitably recompensed for a difficult job was frowned on, to say the least, and you may find that this attitude is not yet out of date.

The National Foster Care Association has always campaigned for realistic rates for foster parents, and annually publishes tables of amounts paid by individual authorities, together with recommendations as to minimum allowances based on the Department of Employment's Family Expenditure Survey. The NFCA stresses that these recommendations are for *minimum* amounts, and certainly as prospective foster parents you should be very wary of authorities whose weekly amounts are less than these. The boarding out rate, as it is usually called, is intended to cover food and extra fuel costs associated with the child, an amount for wear and tear on your household, pocket money for the child and an allowance for clothing (sometimes paid with the weekly amount or sometimes paid as a quarterly lump sum). If the child comes to you with very few clothes, the local authority will pay an 'initial clothing grant', and all basic equipment, such as beds, cots, bedding, prams, extra wardrobes, should be provided. It is worth noting that the weekly amount is usually paid fortnightly in arrears, so, depending on when during the financial fortnight your child is placed, you can sometimes wait a long time for a first payment. (Social workers often find that 'the computer' is a handy scapegoat to blame when money is late!)

Whether or not you are offered a fee on top of the basic payment will depend on many variables, such as which authority you foster for, what sort of child you are looking after, and what schemes for 'enhanced' payments your authority operates. It is fairly common nowadays for those fostering severely handicapped children to be paid a fee in recognition of the fact that such children will be particularly demanding of time. There are also many schemes which recognise the particular skills involved in fostering teenagers by paying an extra allowance, as already mentioned. However, if you are a short-term foster parent, with a great deal of your time committed to the many jobs that such placements involve, you may well find that your commitment and skills are not rewarded financially. Many foster families actually find themselves subsidising the foster child – after all, if you're all going to the local theme park you're not going to leave the foster children behind because the boarding out payment won't cover the entrance fee.

Never be embarrassed to ask about money – you can be sure that every social worker would be on the phone to the finance department the minute they found any discrepancy in their salary! As well as the amounts already mentioned, there are various 'extras' that can be paid, some automatically, others by discretion. For example, grants for holidays, birthdays and Christmas are paid automatically, although two weeks in the Mediterranean isn't usually the sort of holiday the social services has in mind, and a new bike may well exceed the Christmas allowance. Other amounts can be paid for school outings, guide and scout uniforms, music lessons and so on. If in doubt, always ask the social worker what's available.

You should find out from the social worker who's completing your assessment what provision the social services department makes for insuring foster parents. It is possible that foster parents could be held liable for any harm that comes to a foster child whilst he or she is in their care, and also for any damage caused by that child. It may also be the case that foster parents could be made to pay fines incurred by a foster child who has committed an

50

offence. You may find that your household insurance does not cover you for damage to your property by the foster child. You must make sure that you know what your insurance position is, both by contacting your own insurance company and by asking the social services department what cover they provide. Without proper cover you could find yourselves involved in great expense which could have been avoided. The whole matter of insurance is complicated and confusing, and the NFCA have published a very useful booklet explaining it called *Insurance and Foster Care*.

Although the basic boarding out rate is not considered as taxable income by the Inland Revenue, if you are receiving extra payment as recognition that you are looking after a particularly difficult child this money may be liable to tax. Again, this is something which you should discuss thoroughly with the social worker, and you would find the NFCA's leaflet *Foster Care Allowances and Income Tax* very useful here.

CUSTODIANSHIP

Custodianship is a legal status which falls in between fostering and adoption. When foster parents have cared for a child for some years, but adoption is not the plan, it would be possible for those foster parents to apply to a court for the granting of a custodianship order. This would mean that the custodians, as they would then be called, would take on many of the parental rights and duties with regard to that child. For example, they could decide about schooling, holidays, coming-in times and other such details of day-to-day life in a family, without having to refer to a social worker. In fact they wouldn't need a social worker any more, because the child would no longer be in care. The sort of children for whom 'permanent' fostering might be an option may alternatively be candidates for custodianship.

51

Custodianship differs very importantly from adoption in that it only lasts until the child is eighteen, and the order can be revoked or cancelled at any time, on the application of the child's birth parent, the social services department or the custodian(s), provided that the court agrees that this is the right thing for the child. So it can be quite helpful to think about custodianship as a suspension of the rights of the child's birth parents. The custodians have almost total control over the situation while the custodianship order is in effect, but it can be wiped out and the parental rights restored to the birth parents.

Another important point about custodianship is that the birth parents may well continue to have the right to see their children, even if a custodianship order is made, and the court can actually order that access must take place. Often the custodians, the children and their parents are quite happy about this, but there won't be a social worker around to disentangle any niggles between the two families, and if problems do arise they can be hard to solve.

As custodians you couldn't automatically assume that you would receive an allowance for looking after the child, although it is possible for the social services to go on paying an amount similar to the boarding out rate if a child becomes subject to a custodianship order. Alternatively, the child's own parents could be ordered to pay the custodians an amount for upkeep.

As prospective substitute parents you would be unlikely to approach the social services saying that you want to be custodians. A custodianship order is far more likely to be the end product of a long period of caring for one particular child. Further information on the legalities of custodianship are given in Chapter 6.

ADOPTION

Adoption is the most clear-cut way of looking after someone else's child. When the adoption order is made, the child's birth family is legally erased and he or she becomes part of the adoptive family in every sense – he or she takes on their name and family tree as if born to those parents. The child's birth parents no longer have any rights at all over the child. No one can take away the fact that they are the biological parents, but they are not entitled to know where the child lives, who the adoptive parents are, or to make any attempts to contact the child. When a baby is adopted the anonymity of the adopters is important, as it would obviously be upsetting for everyone if the baby's mother knew where he or she lived and risked bumping into the adoptive family in the park or shops. Sometimes a meeting is arranged between the mother (and father, if appropriate) of a baby who is to be placed for adoption and the prospective adoptive parents, who will be referred to only by their first names. The idea is that the mother will find it reassuring to be able to picture the new parents of her child, and the new parents themselves will be able, in later years, to talk to their child about his or her birth mother in more concrete terms. Information about the adopters will certainly be given to the mother, leaving out identifying details such as the area in which they live, their surnames and so on.

There will, however, be situations in which the adopters are known to the birth parents. In the section on fostering the possibility of foster parents adopting their foster child was looked at, and in such a situation it would be likely that the birth parents had been visiting the foster home during the early stages of the placement, and would know their name and address. It may sometimes be thought that the foster parents should not adopt the child simply because the birth parents have such information. This could be a sensible argument if it was feared that the birth parents might attempt to kidnap the child or show violent behaviour towards the adopters, but such extreme behaviour in parents is very unusual and won't often be an argument against adoption.

If you want to adopt a child who has been seeing his or

her parents quite regularly and therefore has clear memories of them, you might meet them during the time before the adoption order is made. If contact between child and parents seems to be a happy experience for both there is, in fact, no reason why this should not continue after the adoption. The adoptive parents would usually have complete control over this, but recently a decision by the House of Lords has made it clear that courts can include in an adoption order a clause which says that an adopted child and members of his or her birth family can go on seeing each other. More common than contact with parents may be contact with grandparents or brothers and sisters who live with other families. Clare, the little girl described in the section on foster parents as adopters, has regular meetings with her grandmother, for example. She enjoys these times and Carol and Vic (her adoptive parents) are quite happy for such contact to continue. Contact between children and their birth families after the making of an adoptive order is still fairly unusual, and many people believe that if such contact is seen as beneficial for the child then custodianship is a more sensible alternative than adoption. The recent House of Lords judgement may mean that these attitudes will change, however.

People wanting to give a permanent home to a child sometimes feel a bit nervous about saying that they will definitely adopt that child before they have all lived together as a family for a while. This is fair enough, and just as no one would want to commit themselves to marriage until they were as sure as possible that the relationship was going to work, you will want to be sure that you and your new son or daughter are going to get along before you ask the judge to make that very final adoption order. It's worth remembering that whilst you can get divorced you can't be 'un-adopted'. The child who comes to live with you may need, very badly, to know that this is where he is going to live for good – and the concept of adoption can be an important one for older children who may have lived temporarily in other families, and who now long for a family of their own.

Before your child moves in with you, you will have got to know him over some weeks or months, will have spent time together on outings as well as doing ordinary family things together, and will have had him to stay in your home. You will also have been given a mass of information about him by the social worker. You'll know his good and bad points, and if he's beginning to feel comfortable with you he may even have paid you the compliment of behaving badly on one of his visits, so that you can get a taste of what life will really be like when he moves in! Hopefully by the time he actually arrives with bag and baggage you will be feeling excited, ready to welcome him as a member of the family, and confident that his stay with you will be permanent. You can tell him all this. You can say that you hope very, very much that you're all going to get along together splendidly and that one day, if everything goes well, you'll be asking the court to make an adoption order. The child can be helped to understand that he has some element of choice in this as well. He should always know who to turn to if he doesn't think all's well in the family, and in this way you will all be able to work together towards the ultimate goal of adoption. As long as the child knows that you *want* the placement to work, that you want him to be with you until he's grown up, he will understand better why, for everyone's sake, you can't say 'we're going to adopt you in six months' time, come what may'.

For some children, however, the making of an adoption order has such tremendous significance that they will be unable to settle properly in their new homes until it has been granted. Children who have been through many moves may find it impossible to really trust their new parents until those parents have shown in a very concrete way that they are totally committed.

During the introductory period and the time when the child is living with you before the order is made, you will have a social worker in the same way as foster parents do. Again you will be part of the team of people reviewing the child's progress with you and trying to find solutions to any problems that may arise. Obviously, then, the whole issue of when is the right time to apply for an adoption order will be fully discussed within this team.

Once the adoption order is granted, many adopters, and adopted children, are only too pleased to say their final goodbyes to the social worker, however well they have all got on. It can be an enormous relief to be able to run your own lives without constantly having to consult the social services department! But if you adopt a child who has had many problems and still behaves in ways that threaten to defeat you, it may be that you will still welcome a relationship with the social worker, even after the adoption order means that the ultimate decisions are yours alone. It is becoming more and more common for social services departments and other agencies to offer 'post-adoption support', recognising that there's nothing magic in a piece of paper and some adopters can feel very isolated if all professional support is taken away at once. As always, this would be a matter for discussion between you and the team, and no one would be expected to force the issue either way.

Finding Out About Birth Parents

When adopted children reach the age of eighteen, the law now says that they can, if they wish, be given information which may make it possible for them to trace their birth families. These days, most adopted people have probably been given such information by their adoptive parents during their childhood, and social workers would encourage this.

As society's attitudes towards adoption have become more open, so the need for secrecy has diminished, and it is recognised that every adopted adult has a basic right to knowledge about his origins. Social workers, who often

56

help those who for some reason don't already have sufficient information, have realised over time that the adopted people who have the most desperate need for more information are usually those who have been told very little about their original families by their adoptive parents. An air of secrecy has hung over the subject and inevitably this has made such people not only more curious about their background, but more prone to unrealistic fantisies about their parents (particularly their mother, since she is the one person most adoptees would dearly love to meet). If, however, adopted children have always been able to talk freely about their first families to their adopters, they will have a more realistic picture of them and their circumstances. They may be able to understand rationally why their mother couldn't care for them, and if they do decide to try to find her they may be better prepared for the reality and less disappointed if the search either draws a blank, or leads to an unsatisfactory meeting.

Adoptive parents have a responsibility to support their children through this process, however painful the experience may be for them. People who adopt children aren't saints, and are bound to have feelings of jealousy and resentment about the child they have loved and cared for throughout his childhood now apparently becoming obsessed with some woman who 'simply' gave birth to him. But it would be foolish not to recognise the importance of this biological fact, and youngsters who can rely on their adopted parents for calm and loving support will cope more easily with what can be a very traumatic process.

For birth parents the word 'adoption' has a horribly final ring to it, and there are few such parents who will give up their children for adoption without many hours of heart-searching. The young mother who feels that she simply cannot cope alone with an unplanned baby can at least console herself with the thought that she is making provision for her child to be happy and well cared for, but this will not prevent her having very mixed feelings about her decision for many years to come. For parents who have tried and failed to look after their children the admission that they cannot manage any longer and would like the children to live with another family must be agonising. Some parents are unable to ever reach the point of saying 'I want someone else to look after my children for good', however obvious it is that the children cannot live at home any longer. Social workers may have to make the decision in such a situation, and it may be against the parents' wishes. It is possible for the courts to make an adoption order without the written agreement of the child's parents. This is regarded as a very serious step, however, and the court would need to hear considerable evidence to prove that the child and parents could not live together. (More information about the legal processes involved will be given in Chapter 6.)

Finance

Most people probably assume that once a child is adopted, there is no further financial help available to the adoptive family. However, it is possible for a local authority to pay an allowance after an adoption, although the actual amount as well as whether or not such a scheme is in operation will vary from place to place. Some years ago legislation made these payments possible, in order to make adoption a reality for children who might not otherwise be adopted because of financial problems. For example, social workers now recognise the importance of finding black families to look after black children, so an allowance might well be available to a black family who wanted to adopt but couldn't take on another child without some extra money. An allowance could also be paid where a family had been caring for a child, wanted to adopt that child but could not afford to do so if the fostering allowances stopped, or in the case of a child who has extreme difficulties, such as handicap. The knowledge of financial back-up might make it easier for a family to commit themselves to such a child.

Adopting a Child from Overseas

Television pictures of sick and hungry children from the third world are very powerful, and it may have occurred to you to look into the possibility of adopting a child from such a situation. Since this book is intended to deal mainly with adoption and fostering in Britain, the subject of overseas adoption won't be considered in detail, but it does deserve a brief mention. (For an excellent look at the whole topic, there is *Everything you need to know about adoption* by Maggie Jones.)

Firstly, most countries trying to cope with famine and poverty prefer to be helped to resolve these problems by the provision of financial and other aid; their children are the next generation, and it could be argued that one would be robbing the country of precious resources in removing a child to an already prosperous nation. Secondly, because there are often no legal regulations governing adoption in these countries the process of bringing a baby home to Britain is always very complicated. If you feel strongly that you would like to investigate the possibility of this sort of adoption, you'll find that you need patience and a determination to succeed, as well as considerable resources to finance trips overseas and so on.

WHEN THINGS GO WRONG

Sharing your home and your lives with a child doesn't always work out. Nobody likes to think of things going wrong, of the placement 'breaking down' (or 'disrupting', to use the social work jargon), but inevitably some placements do end prematurely. Perhaps the first thing to say about such situations is that everyone will be feeling awful. The foster or adoptive parents will feel guilty, thinking that they have failed the child. The social worker will feel worried in case he or she could have done something to save the situation and possibly angry with the substitute family for 'giving up', while the child will be thoroughly confused about what is happening and prob- ably upset about leaving a place and people he loves.

There are all sorts of reasons why placements go wrong, even when the introductory period went well and the first few months were happy and relaxed. When things first start to seem less than perfect, foster parents and adopters can be tempted to bury their heads in the sand, and hope the problem resolves itself without having to admit any difficulties to the social worker. It's always better to *share* your worries at an early state. If your relationship with the social worker is good enough, she won't interpret your need to share problems as a coded request to move the child immediately, and it may be that she can help you through the diffcult patch without the need for a move. On the other hand, if you really have reached the end of the road with a particular child, you have every right to expect the social worker to respond to your needs as well as the child's and to make alternative arrangements for that child's care.

Carol and Vic looked after a brother and sister, Ronnie and Lynne, for two years before they could bring them- selves to admit that Ronnie would have to go. His beha- viour was very difficult, and Carol became so tense that she found herself shouting at him even when he wasn't behaving badly.

'He used to lie under parked lorries in his best clothes, waiting for them to start – nothing you said to him, however you punished him, made any difference. He was self-destructive; he used to stand by the wall outside the house, rubbing his knee against the wall until he'd made a hole in his trousers and then he'd come in and say "Look, I've fallen over". One week he had nine new pairs of trousers! At the time I didn't understand why he was behaving like this, I just thought he was a really naughty boy. We didn't have much help from the social worker. With the experience I've got now, and with a good social worker, I think we would have coped with Ronnie.

60

'I was at my wit's end by the time I said that we couldn't cope any longer, and even then the social worker didn't actually move him for six months – she kept saying "Just try a bit longer". We felt terribly guilty about letting him go, and we still do, even though this all happened twelve years ago.'

This was a very bad experience for Carol and Vic, and doubtless for Ronnie too. It demonstrates how important it is to talk about what's going on – if the social worker had taken the time to really listen to these foster parents she might have been able to find ways of helping Ronnie change his behaviour. At the very least, she would have been able to avoid months of misery and guilt for the family by accepting the need for a move and making arrangements accordingly.

Nobody commits themself to a relationship expecting it to go wrong, and you should be confident at the start of the placement that you and the child can work out any niggles in your relationship. If things don't work, however, never forget the team who are there to share your difficulties and who, after all, shared in the decision to place the child with you in the first place. Guilt is a destructive emotion which can prevent you from helping the child understand what's going on and in preparing him for the move from your home. Nowadays many social services arrange full meetings after the end of a placement, so that everyone involved can have a chance to air their views on the placement as a whole, and discuss what in particular led to the breakdown. Social workers and substitute families alike usually find this process very helpful, with foster parents especially saying how relieved they were to have their opinions and feelings at this painful time fully acknowledged and respected.

If things are going to go wrong in a situation where the plan is adoption for the child, this will usually become clear before the court hearing and the making of the adoption order. However, placements sometimes break down *after* an adoption order is made, and the feelings of failure and guilt are then probably stronger because of the

61

total commitment implied by the adoption order. If you should find yourself in this situation, you'll want to contact the social worker you knew before the child was adopted, if you're not still in touch on a post-adoption support basis. If necessary, your adopted son or daughter can go into care in the same way as any children born to you. Social workers will work with you and the child in the hope that he or she can go back to live with you at some point, and if this is not possible they may even look for another family to adopt the child for a second time. You would remain the child's legal parents whilst he or she was in care, and would be asked to give your agreement to an adoption if this was the plan.

CHILDREN'S HOMES – THE ALTERNATIVE TO FAMILY LIFE

Until fairly recently most of the older children in care, as well as any child who was thought to be particularly difficult to handle, were looked after in chilren's homes. Every social services department and child care organisation would run several large homes, each caring for a dozen or more children.

Nowadays most children in care are fostered, since social workers believe that every child should be able to live in a family. Families have been found to take older children and those whose experiences make their behaviour more difficult to deal with and to understand. Many children's homes have been closed down, but most local authorities still retain a few, as there will probably always be children who can't live in a family for one reason or another. Older children sometimes decide they don't want to make a close relationship with a new mother or father, for example, and the less intimate atmosphere of a children's home suits them better. Perhaps a child may be placed in a children's home after a foster or adoptive placement has gone wrong, to give those working with him or her a chance to think about what sort of family he or she would be most likely to settle with. Finally, there may be an occasion when all the department's foster homes are full, and a placement in a children's home becomes a necessity.

The children's homes that do still exist are usually small, well-staffed units which often specialise in work with a particular group of children, for example, children waiting for the right permanent family to be found for them. They are certainly a far cry from the old-style, large institutions, and can provide a happy and comfortable environment for children who can't live in families.

So, there are important differences between fostering and adoption, and the information here should help you make up your mind which you'd like to consider. Don't fall into the trap of thinking that, since both involve helping children in trouble, they are more or less the same. The two 'jobs' are really very different, and you need to know yourselves and your family very well in order to be able to choose which type of caring would be best for you.

3 The Families

JUDY AND BOB

Judy and Bob have been fostering for about two years. They've got two teenage daughters of their own, and they live in a three-bedroomed council house on an inter-war estate. Bob is employed in the motor trade working a shift system, while Judy is a full-time housewife and foster mother. If you ask them why they decided to go in for fostering, they would find it quite hard to put their reasons into words; 'because we love kids, I suppose, and our own were grown up' is about as clear as they could be on the subject.

They are short-term foster parents, on call one week in four to take children out of office hours. Judy says that most of the children come to her as the result of some sort of family emergency. She very rarely has any advance warning of a placement, and is quite used to a phone call saying 'can you take a couple of kids? I'll be round with them in about an hour'. Judy and Bob regard themselves as a foster family rather than foster parents, and their daughters are often involved in looking after the children placed with them. Bob would be the first to admit, however, that he leaves most of the discussions about the children to Judy: 'She's better at talking to social workers.' Money's fairly tight in this family, but at holidays and at Christmas the foster children are treated like their own, no matter how short a time they've been with them. Judy gets annoyed sometimes about the difficulty of getting extra money out of the social services: 'You have to keep ringing up and pestering them to get the money for a school trip or brownie uniform.' Still, she gets on well with most of the social workers she meets and feels that they do, usually, listen to her point of view.

ANNETTE AND DAVE

Annette and Dave have one 10-year-old daughter of their own. They regret now not having had any more children, but say that they just never quite got around to it and feel that they are too old now to start again with a baby. Annette works part-time as a health visitor; she loves her job and would hate to give it up. Dave's a teacher, and out of work hours both spend a lot of time with youth groups, regularly going on holiday with large groups of youngsters. They've got a very comfortable home, with plenty of room for an extra child.

When they first approached social services, Annette and Dave were quite clear that they wanted to look after another child on a long-term basis, but were not sure whether they actually wanted to commit themselves to adoption. They didn't consider short-term fostering, as they wanted the opportunity to make a lasting relationship with a child. Also, they felt that their life-style, with frequent weekends away and short holidays, wouldn't suit short-term placements. Their daughter, a mature and intelligent child who enjoyed a close relationship with both parents, was fully involved in the decision to foster. The family decided, with the social worker, that their ideal child would be a boy, a few years younger than the little girl, without physical or mental handicap.

Such a lad was identified and placed with this family, but unfortunately the placement didn't work out, despite the undoubted commitment of the whole family to the idea of looking after another child. His behaviour was just too difficult, and caused too much stress within the family for them to continue. After the placement has ended, Dave commented that he hadn't ever felt that the boy's social worker really understood what the problems were, and had been quite unable to offer them any help in finding solutions. The whole family felt very upset and disillusioned when their foster child left them, and haven't felt like risking another placement.

MOHAMMED AND FAIZAL

Mohammed and Faizal were very sad when they discovered that they couldn't have any children of their own. Their doctor suggested that they might consider adopting a child; they thought about this for many months before finally making up their minds to ring the social services department. They were delighted when their application to adopt was taken up very quickly, and they were told that throughout the country there were many Muslim babies in need of adoption, but as yet not that many Muslim couples who want to adopt. When they had been 'approved' as adopters, their social worker sent their details to the British Agencies for Adoption and Fostering, to make sure that they were linked with the first baby who was referred needing a Muslim home. Mohammed and Faizal hoped very much that their baby would be a boy, since sons are very important in their culture. Still, they knew that a baby girl would bring them just as much happiness, and they had made it clear that they wanted to hear about babies of either sex who needed a new start in their sort of family.

Within a few weeks of approval, Mohammed and Faizal were told about Meena, a 3-month-old baby girl whose mother was only sixteen and not in any position to look after her. The mother did not know anything about the baby's father, and he couldn't be traced. They thought hard about Meena for several days before deciding to go ahead. They knew that as soon as they saw the baby they would probably fall for her, and they wanted to sort out their feelings about her uncertain background before their emotions took over. Although they were worried by the fact that nothing was known about Meena's father, Mohammed and Faizal knew that all the babies in need of adoption would have some factor in their history that might worry them, so they asked the social worker to arrange for them to see Meena. As they had thought, they were instantly delighted by her smiles and chuckles, and

Meena came to live with them a fortnight after their first glimpse of her. Five months later she was adopted by them, and now Faizal's only regret is that they didn't contact the social services long ago.

JANE

Jane came to the social services department as a single woman, without any children of her own, who wanted very much to adopt a baby with Down's syndrome. The social worker quickly found her to be a highly intelligent and caring woman who had trained as a nurse for mentally handicapped people. She lived with two sisters, her mother, and the sisters' three children in a tumbledown cottage without gas or electricity in the wilds of the countryside. The children were taught by the sisters at home in an old bus permanently parked by the cottage. Obviously this was by no means a typical adoptive home, but after careful consideration the social worker felt that Jane had a great deal to offer a handicapped baby in terms of time and commitment and such a child was placed with her. Happily this placement has been a great success.

These four descriptions of substitute families should give the idea that there is no ideal or blueprint for foster or adoptive parents. All sorts of people from all sorts of backgrounds look after other people's children. Your own personality and attitudes are far more important than what you do (or *don't* do – many substitute parents are unemployed), where you live and how much you earn. It doesn't matter if you've been divorced (except if you are applying to adopt to certain religious organisations), or if you are single, a man or a woman. The law now also says that couples living together but not married can foster a child, but you would be unable to adopt in this situation – adopters must be either a married couple or single individuals.

WHAT SORT OF PERSON ARE YOU?

What personal qualities do you need to take on this demanding job? Most important is, perhaps, a driving wish to look after another child – not so much a quality as an ambition. This may sound like stating the obvious – presumably nobody will put themselves forward as a substitute parent unless it's something they really want to do. However, it is worth saying, as you do need to be sure about your commitment from the outset in order to survive not only the actual placement but also the demands of the assessment process. A sense of humour usually comes top of many a substitute parent's list of qualities that he or she has found indispensable. Certainly, the ability to see the absurd side of a situation can carry you through and defuse the tension that mounts up with a difficult placement. Tolerance and flexibility are two more qualities that are very important and necessary. You'll have to put up with an awful lot, not only from the children, but also maybe from their parents and possibily even from the social worker – keeping calm will help you survive and look at ways of dealing sensibly with the problems as they present themselves. We've already looked at the sort of disruption a child can inflict upon a family, and an unquestioning rigidity about meal-times and other routines will make you tense and miserable as well as the child.

You'll need to like children and to enjoy spending time with them. Again, this sounds obvious, but many parents who dearly love their own children don't particularly enjoy the company of other people's. Along with this goes the boundless energy that will be essential to cope with the demands of your new, larger family and all the interested ousiders such as parents and social workers.

Marriages or partnerships can suffer badly from the intrusion of another child, particularly an older child who may, as he becomes attached to you, feel jealous of your close relationship with your partner and try to disrupt this.

It's essential that you both have the same strength of need to look after another child and that you understand each other's motives. You need to be good communicators; you won't always have the time to thrash out a misunderstanding between yourselves in private, and will have to rely, rather, on the quickly exchanged word or look. Having said that, if difficulties do arise they must be sorted out between you quickly and without giving the child any opportunity of coming between you. If he can get away with 'playing one off against the other' to his own advantage he'll probably try it!

WHAT'S IN IT FOR YOU?

'Why do you want to do it?' can be a hard question to answer. If you haven't any children of your own the answer will be obvious, particularly if you're applying to adopt a young child. You want to create, by adoption, the family you always wanted naturally. But if you already have children, maybe grown up, the answer will be more complicated and probably harder to explain. 'We love kids' or 'we want to help a child who's less fortunate than our own' are fairly typical responses.

Gloria and Desmond, who have been fostering for more than three years, put it like this:

'We felt that we'd like to give something back; we had three healthy children of our own, who had all benefited from the services provided by the state, such as health and education – we know we're entitled to this because we've paid all our contributions, but we thought fostering was a way of saying thanks for our own family's good fortune.'

Gloria and Desmond are black, and as such they know that they can give something to black children that white couples can't – a sense of their own racial identity and the opportunity to identify with parents of the same background. Black children (in other words Afro-Caribbean and Asian) need to be with people of their own ethnic background. Substitute parents from the black communities are badly needed to look after less fortunate children from these same communities, so if you're black your application to be considered as foster or adoptive parents will be greatly welcomed.

Motivation

In some ways it may not matter very much why you want to look after another child, but it probably is quite important that you work out the answer to this question for yourselves. If you want a child to become a full member of your family, to fulfill a need in you to enlarge your family or to care for a younger child again now that your own are grown up, you may well find yourself disappointed by a child who still has strong links with his own family and doesn't want to commit himself totally to a new mum and dad. On the other hand, if your motives are largely altruistic, or based on the wish to help a child in need, then your satisfaction may come from seeing that child grow in confidence and happiness within your family without ever needing to feel that he is really yours.

Successful foster parents don't have that need to add permanently to their own families – that's not what fostering is about. Their satisfaction comes from seeing a distressed and unhappy child blossom in their care and return again to mum and dad and, hopefully, a more settled home life. Such people will get great pleasure out of their relationships with these children in the short term, but their deeper needs are fulfilled by their long-term and committed relationships within their existing families. Those who want to adopt, however, often feel that there is a real gap in their lives which only another child can fill, and they will do best with children who are ready to commit themselves to the new family without too many regretful glances back at the past.

If you can be honest with yourselves and with the social worker about your motives, you're more likely to end up with a child who'll fit happily into your family. For example, many people really long for a baby and want to experience the physical and emotional satisfaction of caring for a totally dependent child with no direct memories of another family to get in the way of the relationship. If you are one of these people, think very carefully before allowing yourself to be persuaded to consider an older child – even a child of eighteen months has a totally different set of needs from those of a 6-week-old baby. You may have to look at the possibility that you will wait a very long time for your baby, or that you may never get him or her. However, this harsh fact has to be balanced against the other possibility of the misery and disappointment of a placement that doesn't work because your own needs are not being met.

There may, of course, be some motives that social workers will feel they must question. Imagine, for example, a white family with one child, a 6-year-old boy, who have applied to adopt. The couple, particularly the man, longs for a little girl, to the extent that they dare not conceive again in case it's another boy, and to the real detriment of the relationship between father and son. The social worker in such a situation would be right to be concerned about this family's very rigid expectations of a child. Most couples are able to love a child primarily for his or her own self, without being overly worried about the sex of that child. In this case, a girl placed would be the focus of enormous expectations, whilst the couple's own son could feel very hurt and rejected. Another motive which might give rise to concern would be that of providing a natural child with a playmate. There are good reasons, which will be explored later, for avoiding the placement of a child too close in age to a natural child of the family. In any case the natural child and the child placed may not get on. If your child is lonely, it's probably better to try to find children in the neighbourhood for them to play with, rather than seeking to solve the problem through fostering or adoption.

All of us have needs that are satisfied day by day by our relationships, our jobs and our lives at home. Most of the time we don't think much about this, and perhaps you will be surprised by the social worker's wish to concentrate on what you want to get out of fostering or adoption. You may feel that there's some sort of expectation on you to deny that you look for any such rewards, but this isn't the case. Social workers will respect you for being honest enough to admit that you want to look after a child for your own sake as well as for his or hers. An understanding of your reasons will help the social worker decide, with you, firstly whether substitute parenting is right for you, and secondly what sort of children and what sort of placement would suit you best.

YOUR OWN CHILDREN

If you don't have any children or if yours are grown up and away from home, you can certainly be more flexible about the age group and type of child you might look after. Most foster parents and many adopters do have children of their own, however, who will become a very important part of the substitute family and whose needs must be fully considered.

Social workers have a few general rules about placements where there are already children in the home. None of these is hard and fast, however. Firstly, most social workers will be very reluctant to place a child closer in age to your own than two years, although this won't always apply to very short-term placements. At first you may think that another 8-year-old would be ideal, if that is the age of your own child, but there are pitfalls. Your 8-year-old may be big, bonny and bright, doing well at school and with lots of friends and interests. The child who comes to live with you may be smaller, perhaps not very attractive physically, and not doing too well in class. Such a child may immediately feel at a disadvantage when put against your child; they'll probably be in the same class at school, and this would emphasise the difference in their abilities. Hopefully there will be activities that the new child will be good at, perhaps better than your own child, but if they are the same age this can again lead to difficulties and rivalry. If, however, the new child is six, your child can feel grown up by helping him or her along, and won't have the same feelings of rivalry that can be very disruptive in any placement. Equally the new child doesn't have to worry about the fact that he or she isn't as good at sums, or whatever, as your child, because youth permits this lesser ability.

Your own children, also, may not want to include the foster/adoptive child in all activities, but may prefer to be out and about with their friends without the hassle of a new child 'hanging on'. If the ages are too close, it will be more difficult for your children to 'escape'. Although you may wish for them to help the new child settle, it's important to allow them to carry on their own lives, without having to take on too much responsibility for children they don't even really know yet. As the placement progresses, the relationships within the home will sort themselves out naturally in much the same way as in any family of more than one child. However, there will always be situations in which your children simply cannot get on with a particular foster child, and you'll have to decide whether to press on with a divided family or to bring the placement to an early end.

Your own children are used to having you all to themselves, and, depending on their ages, it can be hard for them to have to share you. This is especially so in the early stages when the new child may take up a lot of time. It's important that you talk to your children about all the pros and cons of looking after another child, so that they have some idea of what to expect. It's equally important that they don't feel pushed out by the new child, and you may have to organise your time so that you can spend some with your children alone, without the newcomer. This will perhaps be possible when that child is seeing the social worker or his or her birth parents.

Many foster parents involve their children very fully in decisions to do with fostering, recognising that these decisions affect the children greatly. Carol and Vic, for example, have a family meeting after the end of a placement to discuss whether the family wants another child straight away, and if so, what age group and sex of child would be preferable. It won't always be possible to meet the children's wishes, but at least they have been able to contribute to decisions about their future as a foster family.

OTHER FAMILY MEMBERS

You need to think not only about the effect of fostering or adoption on your own children but also on members of your wider family and your friends. If grandparents are frequent visitors, it's probably going to be a good idea to talk to them about your plans before they are too far advanced. If they have worries about the idea of a 'substitute' grandchild, you can talk this over and hopefully sort out any problems at an early stage. Of course, you may decide to go ahead no matter what anyone says, but again it may be best to know from the outset that granny's not too happy about babysitting for a strange child, for example. Friends are also an important part of most people's lives, so again it's worth knowing their views. They may well be able to help you sort out your own motives and feelings about substitute parenting before discussions start with the social worker.

APPLYING TO BECOME
FOSTER OR ADOPTIVE PARENTS

You've thought about it for a while and decided that you want to go ahead with contacting a social worker and talking about becoming substitute parents. You may be quite clear about whether you want to foster or adopt, or you may want to find out more about the differences before you make up your mind. At this stage what you need is a chat with someone who knows what sort of children there are in your locality in need of homes, and who can answer general questions and help you decide what's best for you and your family. This person will also be able to explain the process of 'assessment', as it's often called – this describes all the meetings with a social worker, group meetings, filling in forms, and so on, that eventually lead to a formal application to be considered as substitute parents.

First Contact

Many people make their first contact with the social services department. This is a department of the local authority which deals with welfare matters affecting not only children and families but also old people, mentally and physically handicapped children and adults, and those who are mentally ill. Many social workers are involved with people from all these groups, although there are some specialists in every field. The specialist in the area of adoption and fostering is often a member of a 'homefinding' team.

There are other agencies dealing specifically with children who also recruit substitute parents – for example, Barnardo's, National Childrens Home (NCH) and the Church of England Children's Society. Initially, such organisations looked after children in large institutions, often orphanages, but nowadays their work is based much more in the local communities, hence the need for foster and adoptive parents. These organisations don't have the same powers as local authorities to take children into care, but often they are asked by the local authority to take over the care of a particular child on behalf of that authority, and this may then mean placing that child with a substitute family. The decision as to where you make your application is entirely yours – a few phone calls will give you some idea of the different ways in which different organisations handle such enquiries, and what sort of time you might have to wait before you can start on the assessment process. British Agencies for Adoption and Fostering publish a very useful booklet called *Adopting a Child*, which lists all organisations, including local authorities, which handle applications to foster or adopt (*see* Further Reading). The National Foster Care Association would also be very willing to advise you on local organisations to contact.

The first phone call to your chosen organisation can seem like a big step – a public declaration of your interest in fostering and adoption. But don't get too worked up – unfortunately, the chances are that you'll be given another number to ring, or told that the social worker dealing with substitute care is out or in a meeting. This is your first taste of the frustrations of trying to get hold of the right person at the right time! Eventually you will get to speak to someone who can advise you correctly, and they will probably ask you for a few very basic details – where you live and whether you're interested in fostering or adoption, whether you're married or single and whether you have children of your own. Some organisations will simply take your name and address and send you some leaflets to look at and a brief form to complete.

The next step may then be a visit from a social worker (appointments are always made for such visits) to talk generally about your interest in looking after a child in care, and to give you some information about procedures and the sort of children who need homes. This is the time for you to ask all the questions that might be in your minds, however trivial they may seem. The social worker may be able to clear them up straight away, or he or she may say 'We'll be covering that in detail in a group meeting or later interview'. Some local authorities and other child care organisations set up meetings for several couples who want to foster or adopt, and this will be your introduction to the organisation rather than a visit from a social worker. Such initial meetings can be very useful, as they enable the social workers to talk to several people at once, perhaps in more detail than would be possible on an individual introductory visit. They also let you see the other people who are also interested in looking after another child, and to listen to their questions – someone may ask something relevant that you hadn't thought of.

After your first contact with the social worker or the group meeting you'll probably be asked whether you want to go ahead with a formal application to become foster or adoptive parents. By this time you will be clearer about which type of caring you feel suits you best. The social worker will ask you to complete a fairly simple form, giving details such as names, date of birth, address, children's names and dates of birth. At this stage you will also be asked to provide the names of two people who are prepared to act as referees for you. They will be visited, usually by the social worker who knows you, and asked what they think about your application to foster or adopt. Obviously these will need to be people who know you as a family pretty well – close friends are ideal. Don't worry about having to find a doctor or a clergyman to give you a reference, since the social worker wants someone who knows you well, and won't be interested in their status.

Checks

The law says that adoption and fostering agencies have to carry out certain other checks on people applying to foster or adopt. There will always be a routine check with the police, as there are some offences which would obviously give cause for concern. You'll be asked to sign an agreement to this police check, and if you have any sort of record it would be wise to share this with the social worker at this point. Many minor offences, such as speeding, will in all probability not affect your application in the least, but it is well to let the social worker know about it. Many organisations also make checks with the probation service, the NSPCC and with your local social services department if your application is not to them. Honesty is by far the best policy here. If you've had any contact with any of these agencies, discuss it with the social worker to avoid complications later. None of these checks will be carried out without your permission, but if you *were* to refuse this permission the social worker would naturally wonder why, and it would probably be impossible to take your application any further. Hopefully the reasoning behind such checks is clear – children who come into care may have had all sorts of distressing experiences, and those involved with them have a duty to ensure as far as possible that they will not be exposed to anyone of doubtful character.

Finally, on the subject of checks, comes the medical. The agency will want you to have a full medical examination with your own general practitioner, firstly to ensure that you don't have an untreated infectious disease that could affect the children you look after, and secondly, to make an assessment of your general state of health. The doctor will supply the agency with a confidential report, which will give details of your medical history as well as your present state of health. The child care organisation's medical adviser will look at this form and advise the social workers on its contents. You won't ever be shown this form, so you may feel like asking your doctor at the end of the examination whether he or she can foresee any problems associated with your application. Social workers do assess medical information with a degree of common sense, and there are no rigid guidelines to say that if you have ever had a particular illness you will not be allowed to look after a child. It's easy to understand, though, that social workers placing babies and young children for adoption want to be reasonably sure that the new parents have a good life expectation. For this reason, a life-shortening illness could affect such an application.

Social Worker Visits

Different organisations have different ways of 'processing' prospective foster and adoptive parents. In all cases, you can expect to be visited in your own home several times by a social worker, and this often forms the main part of the assessment. The social worker will want to get to know you quite thoroughly, so that he or she can assess several different aspects of your motivation and personality. Firstly, there's the simple sharing of information that will be a two-way process between you and the social worker. You will be asked many questions about your life style, background, job, hobbies, children and wider family. You in turn will have the opportunity to ask all about the agency's policy and practices with regard to children, what the allowances are, what training opportunities there are and so on. In this way the social worker starts to get a picture of what sort of person you are, and you also get to know the agency.

Some of the questions you'll be asked won't be factual, and these are always more difficult to answer. You'll be asked about your marriage or partnership, for example, in such a way as to give the social worker an idea of its stability and the way you relate to each other. We can all pick up information about other people's relationships from the way they talk together about ordinary things, but there will be aspects of your relationship that the social worker will ask about specifically. You may have to answer such questions as 'Who makes the important decisions?' and 'What sort of things do you argue about?'. Presumably we would all say we had happy stable marriages if asked outright, especially if we were being assessed to look after other children. For this reason the social worker will frame questions in such a way as to avoid 'pat' answers. Nobody's out to trick you, though, and your social worker should make it clear at the beginning of every interview what he or she is going to focus on and why. If you don't know *why* you're being asked a particular

79

question, say so.

If you're not married or living with a partner, the social worker will probably be interested in your close relationships and how you get support when you need it. A partner is the obvious line of support in times of stress for most people, but close friends and relatives can be just as useful. As a single substitute parent you would certainly need to have people to call on for help of this sort. The social worker will be asking about this primarily to ensure that you wouldn't be too isolated in your new role as foster or adoptive parent.

Your Attitudes

What other areas will the social worker want to discuss? Your attitudes to the children you may care for and their parents will be an important topic. The media often portray the parents of children in care as monsters, particularly when the focus lights on an especially distressing case. Social workers will tell you that most of the parents they see are very far removed from being monsters. They're usually perfectly ordinary people trying to cope with some sort of crisis and unable to be 'good' parents at the same time. Most substitute parents don't regard the parents of the children they look after as a breed apart, but simply as people less fortunate than themselves. They see them, perhaps, as lacking the strength of purpose that goes with being a foster or adoptive parent and carries many of us over life's hurdles. The social worker will obviously want to be reassured that your attitude towards the parents will be sympathetic rather than punitive – if you're a parent yourself it will be easier for you to understand how children can test your patience to its limits.

The social worker will want you to air your prejudices. If you feel that your response to a parent who had used violence against his child could be an urge to black his eye, then this needs discussion, as clearly such a response would not be helpful, either to you or to the child in your care. In theory, many foster parents do feel a revulsion towards violent parents, but in practice the latter often feel so sad and guilty about what they've done that your revulsion turns to pity. As adopters, you will possibly not be faced with actual contact with the child's parents. However, your attitudes are still important, as you will be the ones telling the child about his background, and his self-image will depend, to some extent, on how you describe his parents.

Most people are horrified at the idea of sexual abuse or incest – again, this topic merits full discussion. It's becoming sadly apparent that many children who have suffered other sorts of abuse within the family – physical or psychological – have also been abused sexually. The most common occurrence is father-daughter incest, but sexual activity between mothers and their children of either sex, and between brothers and sisters, is by no means unknown. Many children who are taken into care for totally different reasons later reveal that they have been sexually abused. It's *very* hard for a child to admit to such a thing happening, often because they fear the consequences of telling somebody – dad may have threatened them with a beating or worse if they tell. It is only too possible for substitute parents to have been looking after a particular child for some months, or even years, and then to discover from the child that sexual abuse was going on in their original home ages ago. Adults who are told by children about such activity are often deeply shocked and disturbed, and it can be hard not to react in such a way that the child picks up your disgust and thinks it is aimed at him or her. Don't be surprised, therefore, if the social worker wants to talk in some depth about your attitudes towards sex in order to establish how you might handle such a situation if it should arise. Some children are taken into care because the discovery that they are being sexually abused has been made, and they need protecting. As foster parents of such children you would at least 'know the score', and could prepare yourself for coping with the sort of behaviour that a sexually abused child might display.

Confidentiality

Confidentiality is a very important issue that will certainly be discussed during the assessment process. Any child in care will have a family history that will become known, in detail, to the social worker. The family will be assured that this information will be treated confidentially. They will be told, however, that there are other people who have to know about them and their circumstances, for example, the team leader, doctor, school teacher, health visitor and foster or adoptive parents. We usually think of information given in confidence as remaining with the person we've actually been speaking to, but when a parent of a child in care speaks to a social worker this does not apply. You will be one of several people who know some very sensitive and perhaps shocking information about the child and family, and it's very important that you don't discuss it with anybody outside the child care team. Sometimes it can be hard to keep such information to yourself – through discussion with others we can often clarify information that was hard to digest at first hearing. It's *vital* that such discussions take place only with others on the team, and *not* with your neighbour or best friend. Children will be very hurt and upset if they are taunted about their family circumstances by other children or adults in the neighbourhood, and rumour and gossip fly fast once information has leaked out.

Clearly it's impossible to cover all the topics that the social worker will want to discuss with you, but perhaps these examples have given you some ideas. Some questions will be easy, some will be unexpected, and some may make you feel uncomfortable. Ideally, you will feel that you know yourselves, and all your strengths and weaknesses, better at the end of this process. The social worker will also be more confident that he or she can give an accurate picture of you to the agency.

Group Meetings and Training

For some agencies, group meetings or training sessions will be an important supplement to the individual meetings with the social worker. These will involve a group of people who are also going through the process of assessment as substitute families. By this time you'll know whether you're interested in fostering or adoption, and will take part in a group of similar applicants. Such groups are led by social workers who are well used to work with children and their families, and usually an experienced substitute parent is also involved. If you are invited to attend a series of such meetings, don't worry that you're going to feel as if you are going back to school. The leaders will be keen to get discussion going and will want to hear abour your own experiences. There will be some sessions that will focus on giving you information, but generally the idea is for you to discuss the issues raised with others in a similar situation, and to learn from that discussion and from each other.

Such group meetings will cover a variety of topics. For example, one session might concentrate on the children themselves and their behaviour. Examples of unusual behaviour might be given and ideas about how to handle this sought. Group members could be invited to act out little scenes, taking the roles of substitute parent and child, involved, perhaps, in an argument about coming-in times. Actually pretending to be a child can be a very valuable way of understanding how that child might be feeling. Another session may focus on the child's own family, again attempting to help you understand them by putting yourselves in their shoes. On another occasion the subject for discussion may be the social services department, how it operates, and what you can expect from the social workers you deal with. Films, videos and tapes are often a part of these group meetings, which are usually lively affairs, and much enjoyed by the participants.

Some organisations will make such group sessions a compulsory part of the assessment process. For some they will be optional and others may simply concentrate on individual assessments. If you do get the opportunity of attending such meetings it's well worth taking it up, as you'll almost certainly not only find them enjoyable but very useful as well. Last but not least, you'll meet other like-minded people who could form an important set of friends and contacts when you start caring for another child. Some people are nervous of groups and tend to stay silent. Social workers will be sympathetic, but will certainly try to encourage you to join in as you'll get more out of the meetings if you are an active participant. It's also true that foster and adoptive parents do need, at times, to be able to assert themselves in a group situation – this is a good way of getting some practice! Those organising the groups should always make it clear whether your attendance at them and performance during them counts as part of your assessment, so that you know where you stand. Rest assured there'll be no essays to write, and no exams at the end!

If you have applied to look after a certain group of children with specific needs of their own, such as teenagers or children with mental or physical handicaps, then you may well be asked to attend meetings with these children particularly in mind. Those who want to foster teenagers will almost certainly need and want some guidance at the outset about handling behaviour which will no doubt be difficult and could even be criminal. What do you do if you suspect your teenager is experimenting with drugs? There may be no right or wrong answers to such questions, but by sharing ideas and hearing the experience of others, your confidence to cope will increase.

The concept of training for foster parents has been pioneered in this country by the National Foster Care

Association. This group has stressed for many years the importance of recognising the skills associated with looking after other people's children and has offered training services accordingly. All the other members of the child care team will, almost certainly, have gone through a lengthy training process. Some degree of education, in the form of these meetings, will make you more confident, not only about the job itself but also about your role within that team.

Another useful part of the assessment process can be a chat with a couple who are are already experienced foster or adoptive parents, and many organisations will offer this to prospective substitute parents. You may well find that such people will give you a quite different picture from the social worker, and it's very useful to listen to 'real life' experiences. There could also be questions you feel you can ask people already doing the job that you may not want to ask the social worker. Such a meeting will certainly help to give you a fuller idea of what it's like to take in another child.

A Second Opinion

Finally, you will probably be visited once by another social worker, to provide your assessing social worker with a second opinion. This is a simple safeguard built in by many agencies to try to avoid the possibility that your social worker might have missed something important about you. From your point of view, a different person may give you the opportunity of asking a question you hadn't thought of previously.

The Social Worker's Report to the Adoption Panel

At the end of the period of assessment, the social worker will write a fairly lengthy report, describing you as an individual, couple or family, and giving an opinion on how well you would cope with being foster or adoptive parents. It is now common practice in many organisations for applicants to be shown this report. Many of those in this field of child care feel that it is most certainly the right of applicants to read what has been written about them. This could be something you'd like to ask about at the very beginning of the assessment process – you may like to be sure that your chosen local authority or child care organisation is prepared to be this open with you.

In the case of adoptive applicants, this report now goes before an Adoption Panel, made up of people such as the agency's medical adviser, experienced social workers with and without specialist knowledge of adoption, a member of the social services committee (in the case of a local authority social services department, and meaning a local councillor), and others who might include one or more of the following: probation officer, juvenile court magistrate, child psychologist, experienced adoptive parent, health visitor and teacher. In most cases, applications by prospective foster parents will go before a similar panel for consideration, although the law does not require such applications to be considered in this way. Most social workers would agree that it makes sense for a group of people to look at an application, rather than leaving the decision to one or two people who perhaps already know the family through the assessment process and could be baised one way or the other.

As applicants, you will not be invited to attend this meeting. Generally it is felt that a good, full report, written on the basis of several meetings with you, and backed up by the statements of your referees and the 'second opinion' visit, will represent you and your views in a more rounded way than you could yourself if you were present, faced with a room full of strangers and probably feeling somewhat nervous.

Worries

Fostering and adoption aren't right for every family, and it may be that you start having doubts about your application at some stage in the assessment process. Don't worry or feel that the social worker will be annoyed that you have wasted his or her time if you call a halt. The important thing is to share these worries with the social worker the next time you meet – perhaps you'll find that they can be resolved to your satisfaction and in such a way that you want to continue with your application, or perhaps you will decide to withdraw. The social worker will respect your honesty – it is far better to withdraw early enough than to carry on with unspoken doubts which would eventually lead to unhappiness for you and for any children placed.

Conversely, there will be families about whom the social worker has doubts, and common courtesy as well as good practice dictate that these should be shared at an early stage with the family. There are a variety of reasons why a family or individual may not be considered suitable to look after another child, and if your social worker tells you that he or she has reservations about you, your first thought will probably be 'What's wrong with us?'. In some cases the reason may be straightforward and easy to explain. For example, a family with three children of their own living in a two-bedroomed house will find it very hard to fit in any more children, however keen they may be to help children in need. This family would probably be told on a first visit that their interest was at this stage not very realistic. Similarly, a family with several very young children may not be considered ideal because of the demands of those children, which wouldn't leave enough time for the children placed.

More complex reasons may involve the social worker's opinion about your own personalities or the stability of your marriage or partnership. Most of us will feel upset and probably angry if we believe ourselves to be criticised in this way, and the social worker in such a situation will try to be as sensitive as possible to such feelings in the explanations given. It can be hard enough to go for a job interview and be turned down, but it's even harder to feel you're being rejected when you have revealed intimate and personal details of your life and attitudes. Somehow it feels as if your whole personality and way of life is being called into question. It can help, if you should find yourselves in this situation, to remember that looking after another child *is* a job. The fact that you're not thought to be suitable for fostering and adoption does not mean that you're not a good parent to your own children, nor does it mean that your life-style and set of beliefs is any less right for you just because it isn't seen to be right for another child. Before you part company with your social worker, try to be sure that you understand the reasons why your application is not being taken any further. In this way, you may be able to prevent yourself brooding for too long about what will inevitably have been a distressing experience.

In a very few circumstances it may be impossible for social workers to be totally honest about the reasons for turning down an application. For example, they do not have the right to reveal confidential medical information. If your doctor has formed the opinion that your state of health and medical history make you unsuitable to act as substitute parents, only he or she has the right to give you this information. It may well be that social workers would suggest to doctors that information of this sort should be shared with the patient, but they cannot insist. There may be other reasons which the social worker won't feel able to discuss with you. It would be very cruel, for instance, to say to a couple 'I think your marriage is about to founder'. The regulations which govern fostering and adoption do say, in fact, that no reason has to be given for turning down an application. However, most social workers believe thay have a responsibility to the applicants to explain a rejection if they possibly can.

Turned Down or Accepted?

Very few applicants are turned down by the adoption or fostering panel. It is more usual for the social worker to have discussed his reservations before this stage is reached, and in this case the applicants will probably have withdrawn. It would be your right in such circumstances to insist on your application being seen by the full panel, but many people feel that this is simply a way of prolonging the agony, and would rather call a halt to the application on the advice of the social worker . If you feel strongly that the social worker is unreasonably biased against you, then of course you should contact his or her superior and ask for a discussion with that person. Finally, on this subject, if your application has been turned down by one local authority or child care organisation, think hard before applying to another in the hope that they will reach a different conclusion. Once the second organisation knows that you have made an application to the first (everyone is asked this question when they first apply), they will make contact and check out the reason why it was turned down. There certainly are examples of families who have then been approved by another agency, and if you feel confident in your abilities and sure that the first organisation did not give you a fair hearing then by all means go ahead and contact another agency. You do need a great deal of self-confidence and strength of purpose to weather several rejections, though, so a re-assessment of your motives would be worth while before making any further applications.

Let's hope that your application goes forward to the panel and is accepted. You will be notified of this decision by letter, and will then become 'approved' foster or adoptive parents. Sometimes an adoption panel will, in the same meeting, approve a family as adopters and then go on to agree a match between the family and a particular child – in such a case the family may well have been assessed with that one child in mind all along. In the case of fostering it's more likely that the family will be approved, and then they may have a period of waiting for their first child to be placed. The day of the panel meeting is likely to be a bit nerve-racking, however confident you are about your application, and a phone call from the social worker giving you good news is very welcome!

PRIVATE FOSTERING

If your neighbour were to tell you that her daughter was having problems looking after her little boy, and you were then to agree to look after him yourself for a few weeks while she sorted herself out, you would become a private foster parent. The child would not be in care, so he wouldn't have a social worker, and you would not be an approved foster parent so you couldn't claim an allowance from the local authority. Neither could you turn to a social worker if the placement presented you with any difficulties. Many people do look after children under such informal arrangements, and a great number of them do not realise that they are, officially, 'private foster parents'. Anyone in this situation should tell the social services department that they are caring for a child who is not their own, and a social worker can then visit them and make certain basic enquiries to see that the child is not at risk in this family.

At first sight, it may seem very natural and straightforward to look after a friend or neighbour's child in this way, but it's worth trying to look into the future a bit before committing yourself. The first questions may be about money. Is the child's parent going to pay you an allowance? Who decides how much, and when and how is it paid? What do you do if three weeks go by with no money forthcoming? You should also be asking questions about the length of time the child might be with you, how often the parent will want to visit, who is going to make decisions about clothes and haircuts, how many sweets he's allowed, and so on. Will you go to the parents' evenings at his school or will his mother? The list of questions is endless, and it's down to you to ask them – there will be no social worker to act as a buffer between you and a parent who's suddenly not being very co-operative, or to make sure that your boarding out allowance is there, week in, week out. Many private fostering arrangements work perfectly, but many come badly unstuck, with the private foster parents feeling used and often abused. The above are just some of the issues to consider before taking on this role.

THE CHILD'S RELATIVES AS SUBSTITUTE PARENTS

Sometimes, if grandparents, or aunts and uncles can step in during a family crisis, a child is prevented from having to come into care at all. There will be situations in which the child comes into care and the social worker then discovers that a close relative would very much like to look after that child. In such a case it may be possible to approve those relatives as foster parents, or even to agree to them adopting the child if that should become the plan.

If the relationship between the child's parents and the relative who wants to look after him is good, there may be no need for that child to be in care. The law says that close relatives can look after related children without the involvement of the social services department. In this situation the relatives wouldn't be private foster parents, and they wouldn't have to tell social services what they were doing. Often, however, the relationship with the child's parents is not that good. In this case, grandparents, or aunts and uncles may welcome the involvement of a social worker, who will be able to help them make the best plans for the child's future, and sort out matters of access and so on with the parent.

Most social workers will look very favourably upon the

idea of relatives caring for the child, for obvious reasons. The child will know them, they will be familiar with the family situation, and the child will never feel cut off from his or her family. Such a placement can be particularly right in the case of a child from a minority culture. A Muslim child, for example, may well be best placed within his or her own family, as they will be able to ensure that religious and cultural observances continue to be met. As yet there are few Asian foster parents (such people are badly needed), and it can be very difficult for a white family, however well-motivated, to ensure that a Hindu, Sikh or Muslim child does not become alienated from his or her culture. Afro-Caribbean children can also become quickly cut off from their roots, as indeed can white children. Living with members of their own family can help prevent this.

When the child is in care and relatives are being considered as substitute parents, the social services department will want to assess the suitability of these people in much the same way as unrelated foster and adoptive parents are assessed. Social workers will take account of the fact that the assessment is in respect of this one child only. In the case of relatives offering a child a home, the assessment may well be less time-consuming and intense, given that many of the issues covered in the assessment of non-related applicants will not be relevant. The social worker would certainly want to discuss the relatives' attitudes towards the child's natural parents, for example. However, if one of these parents is your daughter, such a discussion will have a very different slant from one about the parents and the other family with applicants who are strangers. Related applicants will have to undergo medicals, and the same checks will be made with the police, probation, and so on.

There will, of course, be occasions when the relatives are not considered suitable substitute parents. For example, grandparents could feel so bitter about the way their daughter had treated her own child that they would be unable to talk about her in a positive way to their grand-child. They may even find it impossible to have her to visit the child without a row brewing. Such tensions wouldn't help resolve the child's dilemmas about his or her family, and living with non-related foster parents could be prefer-able in such a situation.

Relatives do sometimes adopt their grandchildren, nephews, nieces and stepchildren. Many social workers feel, however, that adoption by relatives 'muddles up' the family tree in a way that can be very confusing to the child. If grandparents adopt, 'nan' becomes 'mum' and 'mum' becomes 'big sister'. These are very hard adjustments for a small child to make and fully under-stand. Grandparents often seek the security of an adop-tion order, particularly if they feel their daughter has been unreliable and uncooperative with them while they have been looking after her child. Nowadays it may well be that custodianship (*see* Chapter 2), can give them, and the child, that security without legally changing the child's family tree.

The adoption of stepchildren by their parent and step-parent, following divorce and a second marriage, is dealt with in law as a separate situation from adoption by relatives or non-relatives. Briefly, if the child in question still has, or even might have in the future, a relationship with the parent she or he doesn't live with, adoption by the other parent and their new partner isn't usually looked on favourably by the courts. Let us take the following situation as an example: mother and father divorce, and the children go to live with the mother, who later remarries. Her new husband wants to make the children legally his own and to give them his name, so they apply jointly to adopt them. The children's father does not see his children because of the bitterness that exists between him and his ex-wife, but he still cares deeply for them and would like to see them again when they are old enough to understand what's been going on. The court reads the social worker's report and hears that the

93

natural father is not prepared to give his agreement to the adoption of his children. The decision is that they should not be adopted because of the father's lack of agreement, and the possibility that a relationship between him and his children could be re-established. Sometimes fathers in similar situations actually give their agreement to the adoption of their children, perhaps because they can see no way round the bad feelings. The court could still refuse, however, to make an adoption order, for the same reasons. If an adoption order is not granted, it is usually possible to ask a court to change the custody order (which would have been made at the time of the divorce), so that it now includes the mother's new husband as a person who has legal custody of the children.

You may have noticed that the natural mother and stepfather have to apply *jointly* to adopt the children. If the stepfather were to apply alone, an adoption order would exclude the mother, as all parental rights would then belong to the stepfather. So a joint application has to be made, and the child's birth mother would, if an order is granted, become in law that child's adoptive mother. There are still occasions when adoption orders can be made in these situations, if, for example, the natural father makes it quite clear that he wants nothing more to do with his children, or perhaps if his whereabouts are unknown.

You may well be feeling surprised and perhaps a little alarmed at the nature and depth of the enquiries that are made during an application to foster or adopt. Obviously the major reason is to protect the children who are in care. They have already been through difficult times, and social workers must be sure that placing them with new families will not in any way put them at further risk. This is no ordinary job, and the selection process is more than an interview – and so it should be. This process is also a safeguard for you, the prospective foster or adoptive parent. The experience of a placement that goes wrong is devastating in any circumstances, and if you feel it's gone wrong because you weren't properly prepared for the task, you'll feel even worse. Finally, many people thoroughly enjoy the social worker's visits and the group meetings, and find themselves able to embark on the actual business of living with other people's children with confidence and enthusiasm.

4 The Child's Own Family

When you first start to think about looking after another child, you may not consider the parents and other relatives of that child. Certainly, the idea of having them frequently in your home as a part of fostering won't be uppermost in your mind, but a child's contact with his parents while he is away from home is one of the most important aspects of fostering. It is also one of the most difficult to manage. For would-be *adoptive* parents, the subject of contact with the child's family is very different, and will be looked at quite separately.

ACCESS

Face-to-face meetings between children in care and their parents are usually called 'access' meetings or visits. Social workers will talk about parents being 'allowed access' to their children. Other forms of contact can also be very important, such as the exchange of letters, telephone calls and photographs. The word 'access' will only be used to describe actual meetings, however.

The child care team will be looking at plans for access at the beginning of every placement, and such plans will vary according to the age of the child, how long the placement is likely to last and the overall goals. If you have a 2-year-old living with you for a few weeks, the overall plan being to return that child home as soon as possible, access between child and parents will need to be very frequent. It is essential to keep alive those all-important bonds of attachment. Very young children forget quickly, and time, as expressed in a statement like 'Mummy's coming to see you next Tuesday', has no meaning for them. In such a situation children probably need to see their mother (and father, if possible) almost every day. She needs to stay in their minds as the most important person in their lives, and her role must not be allowed to be taken over by the foster mother.

This frequency of access will keep alive the bonds that cement the parent-child relationship, and will probably result in the children being upset after every visit from their mother. They won't like to see her go, and may behave in ways that are upsetting for you and possibly difficult to handle. Adults don't like to see children distressed, and it can be tempting to consider stopping the visits that seem to be the cause of that upset. But consider your own feelings in a similar situation. Imagine yourself in hospital – your nearest and dearest comes to see you often, and you hate it when they go, but because you have an adult's control over your feelings you put on a brave smile. What if they suddenly stopped coming? Not only would you be devastated at the total lack of contact, but you'd probably wonder if you had done anything that had put them off visiting. Your distress might show for a few days but eventually you would resign yourself to this lack of contact with the upset hidden away inside. As an adult you can deal with such feelings. You can tell yourself rationally that you can't possibly have caused your partner to stop visiting, and that there must be some good reason why he or she isn't there. A child can't work things out in the same way, and small children will be upset evey time their mother and father leave, because they can't grasp the idea that they will be back tomorrow or the next day. If the adults concerned decide to stop the parents visiting because the children are distressed, this will have a very serious effect on the relationship between parents and child, although it may get round the prospect of the child screaming at every parting.

It can be tempting to take the line that a small child should be allowed time to settle in the foster home before access to the parents is set up. This, again, can be more convenient for the adults, but is no good for the child. After some initial period of upset, he or she may appear to settle in without any contact with his or her parents, but will in fact be deeply disturbed by not having seen them. When they do finally visit, the child may appear reserved and even angry with them, because the bonds of attachment and affection will have been seriously weakened by this time without any contact. You will have plenty to do in the early stages of placement, but it's vital not to let too many days go by before parents and child meet. If the social worker doesn't seem to be making arrangements for this, it's your job to ask him or her what's going on, and to voice your opinion that an access meeting should be arranged.

Older children still have the same need to see their mother and father quickly, for obvious reasons. They'll be upset following the reception into care and will want to reassure themselves that their parents are all right, and to know where they are. They need to be confident that their parents know where they are living. Older children can be told and can understand that mum and dad won't be visiting until Sunday (or whenever), and they can hold on to the fact that their parents still love and care for them, even though they can't live with them at the moment. Consequently, access doesn't need to be as frequent as for a younger child. The important point here is that both children and parents should know as soon as possible after placement when and where they can see each other, and that plans made should take into account their wishes.

For some children, access to parents and other relatives can be fairly infrequent, possibly during school holidays only. This might work in a placement that eveyone knows is to be long-term, and where children will not be returning to their families. In such a situation, children gain pleasure from this contact with members of their original family, whilst being quite clear in their minds that they won't be going back to live with them. The occasional contact helps the children keep a sense of their own roots without making them feel any less wanted by their foster parents.

Practicalities – Time and Place

Everyone involved in access needs to know when and where it's going to happen, including the foster parents. Children are usually most comfortable in familiar places, and it may well be, therefore, that most of the access meetings will take place in the foster parents' own home. It would be wrong to suggest that this is an easy situation for foster parents to cope with, particularly when parents are visiting often, and perhaps for half a day at a time. Carol and Vic were in a similar situation when they first fostered Clare, the little girl they eventually adopted because she couldn't go home. Her mother used to visit three days a week, from 9 o'clock in the morning until 9 o'clock at night, and during that time she would take total charge of Clare. Carol would leave the two of them together in the living room while she got on with other things. Clare's mother had physically hurt her daughter, and she was having to re-learn how to be a parent, and how to handle a small child without losing her patience to the extent that she had in the past. Later on she was able to take Clare out to her own flat, but in the early stages she simply couldn't be trusted with the child and had to stay at Carol's. Obviously, these day-long visits made a big difference to Carol's life, but luckily she liked Clare's mother and she was very keen that Clare should go home when the time was right. As Vic said:

'The work we did with Clare's mum and dad was really an extension of our fostering – in a way we were fostering them as well. We were very happy to be doing this work – we got on well with the parents and wanted Clare to be able to go back to live with them.'

Sadly, when Clare did return home things still didn't work out, and eventually Carol and Vic adopted her. But at least they know that they tried their best, with the social worker, to give Clare's parents every opportunity to maintain contact with their child, and to learn how to look after her properly.

Sometimes foster parents can actually show birth parents how to look after their child in a way that won't lead to a loss of temper or be neglectful of that child's needs. Perhaps you're fostering a toddler, and his mother says he gets into terrible temper tantrums which she can't control and which make her very tense. If you're both in the room when one of these tantrums starts up, you could show his mother how you handle them – perhaps you distract the child, or you simply calmly ignore his screaming until he quietens down. If you, his mum, and the social worker have previously agreed that you may be able to help by showing how you handle different behaviour problems, she may find it very useful to follow your 'model'.

Sometimes it's just not possible or practical for parents to see their children in the foster home, and there may be various reasons for this. To take an extreme example, if there is a real danger that the birth parents could try to remove their children, or harm them in some way, or attempt to cause injury or damage to the foster parents or their home, then the social workers may decide that those parents should not be told where their child is living. Access in these situations would take place somewhere else – possibly at a nearby children's home. These situations should be very unusual. As a general rule, birth parents have a right to know where their children are, and it will be very hard for the children not to reveal an address when they see their parents. So, before taking such a drastic decision with regard to any child, social workers should be very sure why it is they're not prepared to trust birth parents with the address of the foster home.

In other cases, parents simply cannot cope with the idea that someone else is looking after their child, and just don't want to face the foster parents on an access visit.

Meetings with the child could take place somewhere else –
maybe even at the home of another foster parent –
perhaps for a temporary period, while the birth parents
accustom themselves to the idea that their child is in care.

By and large, short-term foster parents *will* have to cope
with frequent visits from parents and the accompanying
disruption to routine. This doesn't mean, however, that
your own need for time on your own and privacy won't
be respected. Access visits should always be by prior
arrangement, either directly between yourselves and the
parents or through the social worker. Unexpected visits
can sometimes be tolerated, but if a parent should turn up
unannounced at an inconvenient time it's perfectly all
right to explain this and make another arrangement.

THE PARENTS' FEELINGS

Most parents will feel angry, upset, and above all guilty
about the fact that their children are in care. They
probably want them back desperately, and may not totally
understand what's going on, particularly if the courts are
involved. They'll be unusual if they don't have some
feelings of resentment about the fact that you, total
strangers, are looking after their children. All these feelings can mean that it's very hard for them to visit their
children, much as they want to see them.

It's up to the social worker and the foster parent to do
everything they can to encourage parents to visit. The
social worker can make sure the parents can afford the bus
fare to the foster home – financial help can be given to
parents if this is a problem. Ideally, the parents will have
met the foster parents before the children go to live with
them, but if not the social worker should certainly accompany the parents on at least the first visit to make introductions, and to ensure that they know how to get there. Once
the mother and father are in your home there are many
small things you can do to make them feel welcome, and it

really will be up to you to make the effort. Most parents will want to see their children on their own, and you'll have to make sure that there's a room that's warm and comfortable where parents and children can relax. The parents may well be feeling nervous, and perhaps the child shares this feeling. You can help them by chatting about what's been happening in the child's life, and most importantly by involving them in doing something for or with the child. There's usually no reason why a mother shouldn't feed and bathe her baby, for example. Parents of toddlers could prepare a meal and then help with bath and bedtime, and older children could have a favourite activity such as drawing or reading to share with their parents. It's important to avoid a situation where parents and children are just sitting in a room with nothing in particular to do, as most families don't spend that much time sitting and talking face-to-face. Chats are much more likely to occur over some shared task. It's well worth thinking ahead, and setting up something that can be done together by parents and children, at the same time avoiding, as much as possible, feelings of artificiality. The child's social worker should be able to help with some ideas of tasks that can be shared when parents visit.

Some parents won't turn up for visits no matter how hard you and the social worker have tried to encourage this. The disappointment on a child's face when mum doesn't arrive at the arranged time is hard to cope with, and it's natural to feel angry at her for causing this unhappiness. Try to hide your irritation from the child. Talk calmly and sensibly about what might have happened to prevent mum visiting, and offer reassurance that she will still be welcome the next time. Take time to think about why visits are being missed, and to discuss this with the social worker; don't let time drift by with too many missed visits before the issue is tackled with the mother, perhaps by you and the social worker together. Perhaps the child could be encouraged to write a letter or draw a picture for her – this might help her to feel needed and to

102

overcome her own anxieties about visiting. Certainly you can help keep mum alive in a small child's mind by talking about her and looking at photographs of her together. The child will feel worse if you suddenly stop talking about mum, or don't say when she will be visiting next.

If you're black, you can probably imagine that for black parents the idea of visiting their child in a white foster home might make them feel very uncomfortable. Black foster parents would be tremendously helpful here as they would be able to make the black parents feel welcome in a way that white foster parents could never manage, however good their intentions. The child would see that his or her parents were getting along well with the foster parents, and access would be off to a good start already. If the social worker is white, then you as black foster parents would be able to help him or her by indicating the best way of welcoming the parents and helping them relax. The way we react to strangers when they visit our homes is to some extent dictated by our culture, so it's obvious that a Sikh foster couple, for example, will be in the best position to respond to Sikh parents.

THE RELUCTANT CHILD

Most children will look forward to visits from their parents eagerly. Some children will be less enthusiastic, however, and some may even refuse point blank to have any contact. You and the social worker will have to read between the lines here, and be open to small signs that children don't always say what they mean. Older children who have been badly treated by their parents may be quite genuine in their unwillingness to see them. Of course, their views must be respected, but if there is to be any possibility of them returning home, bridges must be re-built to allow for access to take place. You and the social worker will both want to talk to such children about what's happened at

103

home, and the social worker, who is in touch with the parents, can perhaps reassure them that their mum and dad do still love them and want to see them no matter what's happened.

When small children appear reluctant to see mum and dad, this may just be a reflection of their feelings of confusion about what's been happening to them over the past few days or weeks. Obviously if they show real signs of fear or distress during a meeting with parents this has to be taken seriously and the causes assessed.

WHEN ACCESS HAS TO BE STOPPED

In certain circumstances the social services department can, with legal back-up, prevent parents from having any contact at all with their children. This is a very serious step, and one which is only contemplated if it becomes clear that access is no longer helping the child. For example, if parents go on and on missing visits, despite every encouragement, then the child care team may have to decide that this, combined with other signs of the lack of a real wish to have the child back home, means that a family which can look after the child permanently should be found. Once the decision that the child should be placed with adoptive parents has been made, it doesn't usually make sense for access to continue, and the parents would be told that they no longer have the option of visiting their child. Occasionally access is stopped because the child is badly upset by parents' visits, but it should be emphasised that such a decision will only be taken in extreme cases. (*See* Chapter 6 for more details about the law on access.)

FOSTER PARENTS' FEELINGS

It's been said before, but it's worth repeating: you will probably find the whole business of access one of the most difficult and upsetting aspects of foster care. The most important thing is to remain aware of your feelings and how they affect your actions, for you have enormous power in this situation.

Imagine the following: you're looking after a 4-year-old, Katie, and the plan is that she should go back home to mum and dad when they've been able to convince the social worker that they can look after her without either losing their tempers or neglecting her. The parents visit twice, sometimes three times, a week, causing you quite a bit of inconvenience. The father is a heavy smoker, which you don't like, and the mother seems to spend most of her time sitting in a chair and not taking much notice of her daughter. However, there's no denying the affection that exists between the parents and the little girl, who always cries bitterly when they leave. One week they only come to visit once, and, to be honest, you breathe a sigh of relief at having the house to yourself on the occasion of the missed visit. Katie is upset when they don't turn up, and you comfort her by promising her a treat. You've become very fond of Katie over the few months that she's been with you, and you're angry with the parents for upsetting her. The next time they are due to visit you don't tell Katie just in case – and you later feel you did the right thing because they don't arrive. That night, at bedtime, Katie tells you that she loves you more than her real mother.

When the social worker calls you tell her about the missed visits. She's concerned and says she will visit the parents that day to find out why they didn't visit as arranged. When she's gone you feel awful, as you admit to yourself that you don't want them to visit – in your heart of hearts you think Katie would be better off without them. But the social worker discovers the problem was simply one of illness, and the visits start again. Despite your best intentions, you're not quite so welcoming, and when Katie becomes a bit confused about which mummy to go to, you find it hard to encourage her to sit on her 'real' mother's knee.

105

As a foster mum in this situation you have fallen into an easy but dangerous trap, and need to examine your own feelings quickly and carefully with the social worker. By your attitudes towards the parents and Katie, you're starting to give out the message that you aren't too keen on access and that *your* relationship with Katie is as important as Katie's ties with her parents. Children are very sensitive to adults' feelings, and Katie, who has naturally become fond of her foster mother, will almost inevitably start to respond to this change of attitude and become confused about her feelings for her own mum and dad. For their part, her parents will find visits more and more difficult if they don't feel welcome and don't receive the same degree of affection from Katie. They may well start to miss visits or stop coming altogether.

The social worker can't understand why access isn't working as well as it was. The plan is still for Katie to go home, and the foster mother can't give any reasons against this, but the social worker senses that all is not well. Now is the time for you as the foster mother to be honest enough to admit not only your feelings of irritation with the parents, but also your growing affection for Katie. If you don't, you could quite easily jeopardise the plan for the child to return home by your attitudes. A straightforward talk with the social worker, and possibly then the parents as well, may help to sort out a difficult situation, and hopefully you will be able to recognise that you have been in danger of misusing your power in this situation.

The moral of this tale is very simple: you must examine your own feelings carefully and frequently, and if you find yourself wishing the parents would stop visiting, contact the social worker and talk this through. It may be that your feelings are right and visits are no longer helpful to the child. However, your very understandable wish to protect the child from pain may also have prevented you from being coolly objective about the situation, and steadfast in your support of the plan for the child to return home.

It's not hard to imagine that the issues raised by Katie's story would be much more complicated if Katie was a black child in a white foster home. Her parents might well start off with uncomfortable feelings about the white foster mother, and the child's feelings of uncertainty about whether to respond to her own black mum or the white foster mum to whom she had become attached could lead to great confusion about her racial identity. A black child in this situation could easily become unhappy with her colour and start to fantasise about being white.

Take comfort! There will certainly be other children whose parents you like and get on with, and have no difficulty in welcoming into your home. You'll be genuinely pleased to see these families reunited and will have used your power positively in such a case.

OTHER RELATIVES

Whilst the mother and father are usually the most important visitors for a child in care, there may well be other members of the family who want to keep in touch with their young relations. Brothers, sisters and grandparents are perhaps the most obvious examples. It's often easier for the foster parents to welcome members of the wider family into their homes, and indeed easier for such people to visit. The feelings of guilt and anger carried by the parents won't be there – at least not to the same extent.

Grandparents can have a very important part to play in children's lives, and if your foster children talk warmly about nan and grandad, you could discuss with the social worker the possibility of regular contact. If the social worker doesn't know the child very well you may be the first to hear that grandparents are around and that the child would like to see them. Brothers and sisters may visit with mum and dad, or, if they are also in care but with different foster parents, regular outings could be arranged to include the whole family.

ACCESS IN CUSTODIANSHIP AND ADOPTION

The possibility of some contact between children and their birth families after the court has made either a custodianship or an adoption order is an issue which should be considered in some detail.

Most children who become the subject of a custodianship order are living with foster parents or relatives, and already see one or more members of their original families on a regular but perhaps not very frequent basis. Usually the people applying for a custodianship order are quite happy for this access to continue. Originally it was probably arranged through the social worker, but now it may well be that the foster parents and the child's relatives make contact during school holidays, for instance, and arrange a meeting or an outing. Kerry is a 13-year-old girl who comes from a large family of five children. Her two little sisters live with a couple who have adopted them and Kerry doesn't have any contact with them, but her two older brothers live at home with mum and she enjoys seeing them when they're all on holiday. Kerry's foster parents are quite happy about these occasional trips out, and they are applying for the custodianship order on the understanding that this contact will continue. Kerry has decided that she does not want to see her mother, not having lived with her for several years, and everyone agrees that Kerry should be allowed to make up her own mind on this point.

Kerry's situation is settled and happy, and probably fairly typical. However, if you're considering applying for a custodianship order you should certainly think about whether there will be any contact between the child and the birth family when the order is made, not forgetting that the court can *insist* that this should happen. Think about which family members are going to carry on seeing the child. Do you get on with them reasonably well? Do you already make the arrangements for access, or do you rely on the social worker to sort this out? Have there been any problems with access, such as missed appointments or arguments about dates and times? Do you really want the child to go on seeing these relatives? If you have doubts, and would feel anxious about making arrangements yourself rather than leaving this to the social worker, this should be discussed with the social worker before your application is made to the court. If the court makes a custodianship order, with a clause saying that access must continue between the child and its mother, father, or whoever, you're on your own. The child will no longer have a social worker to sort out any misunderstandings between you and the relatives. If you and the social worker reach the conclusion that access arrangements could easily go wrong and cause problems for you and the child, it may be that you should not make the application for a custodianship order but should carry on as foster parents.

When relatives of the child apply for a custodianship order the position will obviously be quite different. The child's relatives are, after all, also his or her family. Usually any contact between child and parents (or other family) will happen naturally as a part of life with the custodians, whether they are grandparents, aunt and uncle or whoever.

When a court makes an adoption order it can also state that access to some member of the child's family should continue. Until fairly recently adoption was considered to be the final and total break with the child's birth family, and in most situations this will still be the case. Most adopters and children want to start afresh with a new family tree, and would find continuing contact with birth relatives upsetting and confusing. In fact, courts have refused to make adoption orders in situations where there is still any access, preferring that that final legal break with the original family should not be made. However, recently this view has started to change, and courts are recognising that children can benefit from the 'best of both worlds'. They can be given the total security of an adoption order but can still enjoy seeing a brother, sister or grandparent. It could be said that such children are lucky enough to be members of two families! (*See* Chapter 2 for more on this, particularly comments on a recent decision on access after adoption made in the House of Lords.)

Whereas a child on a custodianship order could still go on seeing a parent, it seems unlikely that access to a parent would continue after an adoption order. Most courts would take the view that adoption, with its final severance of legal relationships between child and family of origin, would not be the right course for a child who still enjoyed contact with mother or father. After all, custodianship can be revoked, and it is still possible that the natural parents could once again look after the child. Parents are certainly not cut off in the way that they are following an adoption order.

GOLDEN RULES

By now you may be tired of hearing that looking after other people's children is hard work, but it can't be repeated too often. Coping with access is one of the hardest aspects – everyone's emotions are so fully involved, yet for it to work properly arrangements need to be made with a calm objectivity. Perhaps it would be helpful to end this chapter with a few 'golden rules'.

1 Babies and pre-school children particularly need to see their parents *quickly* and *frequently*. Be insistent with the social worker if this hasn't happened within two or three days of placement.
2 All children need to know when and where they will be seeing mum and dad. There should always be contact within the first week of placement and plans made for timing, place and frequency of future contact.
3 You should know what's going on, so the access plan should be written down and kept safely for you to refer to.

4   Parents should be quite clear about arrangements. Financial help can be offered by the social worker for bus fares and other expenses.

5   Be aware of your feelings, and discuss them with the social worker.

6   Try to make allowances for the parents – think about how you would feel in their position. Help them to feel welcome by finding something they can do with and for their child, and don't think the worst if they miss a visit.

7   Make sure your house is still your own! Be clear with the social worker and the parents that certain times are for your family only – Sunday mornings if you are church goers.

5 Social Workers

THE ORGANISATIONS

The social services department is a part of the local authority in every area, whether county council or metropolitan borough. The law of the land states that each local authority must have a social services department (this term will be used to cover social work departments as well), and there are many acts and other pieces of law which lay down what sort of work these departments should take on. Social services departments haven't been in existence for very long. Many people will still remember the days of the 'welfare', before the terms 'social services' and 'social worker' became common. In fact, social services departments were established in the early 1970s, and brought together several departments which used to deal separately with the elderly, the handicapped, the mentally ill and children. The idea was that any family with difficulties should be able to go to one single department and know that all its problems could be handled under one roof.

Nowadays the social services department is a large organisation employing thousands of people with all sorts of different skills and backgrounds. The director of social services has ultimate responsibility for his or her department, and below them will be a variety of personnel with responsibility for different areas of work, who may be called deputy or assistant directors, area or district managers or principal officers. It's impossible to give a blueprint to cover the organisation of every social services department, as no two will be exactly alike. In some cases, for example, the department may be divided into sections dealing broadly with residential care and work in the community (often known as 'field work'). Other departments will split up responsibility on a geographical basis so that the manager of a small area will look after *all* the facilities, including children's homes and old people's homes, in that particular place. People's titles can be very confusing – the district manager of one department may have a job that is quite different from that of another person in another department who might also be called 'district manager' – in the second place the 'area officer' might do the same job as the district manager in the first department!

If you become substitute parents for a social services department it's important that you have some idea of the structure and set-up of the department, and sometimes this is covered in training sessions. Most of the time you won't have anything to do with the senior management of the department, but if you at least know how the organisation works, you'll be in a better position to appreciate where the social worker fits in. Perhaps more importantly, you should know who to approach if you're dissatisfied with the service you're receiving from the department.

The people who actually have most face-to-face contact with the public are usually called 'teams' of social workers, run by team leaders. Again, different departments organise these teams differently. One possibility is a set-up with teams which deal with different groups of people in need. The 'general services' teams will deal with all problems as they first come to the department's attention, and if further work is needed the case will be passed on to a more specialist team. This second team may only take on work with children, or old people, or the handicapped, or the mentally ill. In this way the first point of contact is the same for everybody, but if the family or individual need specialist help, this can be made available. In this particular case the authority will also have teams of social workers who specialise in fostering and adoption work. These are called 'homefinding teams'.

Alternatively, the organisation might be as follows. The social workers will be divided up into teams, but each team will deal with all the problems thrown up by its own small geographical area. A social worker in the team could be dealing with various situations during any one week, although even within this type of team there may be individuals who tend to work with children, and others who concentrate more on the elderly, for example. An authority organised in this way would probably also have established specialist homefinding teams, and the fact that many social services departments recognise the need for separate teams to deal with fostering and adoption will give you some idea of how important this area of work is considered to be.

As yet there are not very many black social workers, but their numbers are increasing. Those in charge of the homefinding teams are very keen to recruit black social workers as they know that prospective foster and adoptive parents who are themselves black will find it much easier to talk to someone who shares their culture. It might be worth finding out whether you could be visited by a black social worker if you're black yourself, as this might influence your decision about which child care agency to apply to.

Work with children takes up an enormous amount of 'social worker time', and work with the elderly is also very time-consuming. Most people are probably aware that the proportion of the population who can be called 'elderly' is growing all the time, and consequently social services departments have to cater for their needs in ever-increasing numbers. Every local authority runs many elderly persons' homes, and employs hundreds of home helps who are invaluable in helping old people stay in their own homes if this is what they choose. Some authorities have set up schemes for finding families who will foster an elderly person. Perhaps if you find that other people's children don't fit in with your life-style, you could think about looking after other people's grannies and grandpas!

Social services departments have certain legal rights in

relation to children in the area which they cover. There are also several big child care organisations which, although they don't have the same powers, are allowed to make arrangements for the care of children and sometimes for the adoption of those children. The fact that you could decide to approach one of these organisations as prospective substitute parents has already been mentioned. Barnardo's is perhaps one of the best known of such organisations, but there are several other large national charities working in the field of child care, notably the Church of England Children's Society and NCH (previously called National Children's Home). Don't be put off by the titles – you don't have to be a member of the Church of England to approach the Children's Society, as it is more usually known, and NCH now has a far wider scope than simply running residential establishments for children. As well as these major organisations, there are large numbers of local children's charities, often Catholic in orientation and often dealing with the placement for adoption of the babies of Catholic parents. Most of these local organisations do have a religious base, and may not be prepared to consider people who are not largely in sympathy with their Christian philosophy. Some will go further and accept applications only from those who are members of the church in question, for example, Catholic.

Because these organisations only deal with children and their families they are obviously much smaller than local authority social services departments and all the social workers will be specialists in the area of child care. There will almost certainly be groups of social workers dealing specifically with the placement of children for fostering or adoption. These organisations don't take children into care themselves, but the social services department can ask an organisation to take on the job of finding a family for a particular child in its care. In practice the 'voluntary' (as opposed to statutory) organisations often take on work with children whom the social services department have found especially difficult to place with families. So, if you're thinking about approaching one of these agencies it's worth bearing in mind a couple of points – they won't be looking for short-term foster parents, as short-term and emergency care will be dealt with by the social services department, and the children for whom they are seeking long-term or permanent homes will probably have some particular difficulty. They may have a handicap, or simply be over a certain age, both of which will make finding the right family less easy.

SOCIAL WORKERS

You'll have gathered by now that a social worker may be a 'jack of all trades', or a specialist working in a particular field. As a substitute parent you may find yourself dealing with one or more of each. All children in care have their own social worker, whose job is to work with the whole family, not just with the child in care. He or she may be part of a team working with the whole range of people needing help or only with children and families. Every social worker brings his or her own personality and experience to the job. Some will have many years of experience, and may have children of their own, whereas others will have just finished their training, and will be young and full of enthusiasm. Obviously, you will like, and get along with, some better than others, but it's best not to jump to conclusions about someone before they've had a chance to prove themselves. The young man who's only been in the job a matter of months may be just as good at listening to your problems and offering helpful advice as the middle-aged woman who has children of her own and years of experience in child care. On the other hand, she may be better than he is at talking football with 10-year-old boys because her own son is an ardent fan!

Whenever you have a child living with you, you will be visited regularly by that child's social worker. You may also receive less regular but very important visits from a specialist social worker, who will want to talk with you about more general aspects of substitute care. Your relationship with both these social workers is going to be a major factor in your feelings of satisfaction as a substitute parent, and in the success of any particular placement, so it's worth looking at this issue in some depth.

General attitudes are crucial. Social workers should approach you as a valued colleague, with whom they are prepared to share all the information they have about the child you are, or will be, looking after. As the placement progresses, your opinions and observations concerning the child should be respected and taken fully into account by the social worker and the rest of the child care team. For your part, your attitude should show that you see yourself as having a very important part to play in the child's life and in planning his or her future. The social services department, or child care organisation, has publicly stated that you are a very competent person to look after other people's children, and this gives you a status equal to that of the social worker in any discussions about those children. In other words, don't be intimidated by the bulging diary and harrassed expression!

Making Best Use of Visits

The child's social worker will visit you before the child comes to live with you, to tell you all about the child and look at the plans for the placement. You and the social worker will want to plan when, and how often, he or she will be visiting once the child is with you, and to talk about the purpose of those visits. How often you and the social worker meet will depend on such matters as how well the child has settled with you, and what's happening with his or her own family. Any problems will almost certainly lead to more frequent visits which will be used to try to sort them out. At the beginning of any placement, most social workers would want to visit very quickly, and then probably weekly or fortnightly for the first few weeks. Make your own feelings clear when you're discussing the timing of visits. If an occasional evening appointment when all the kids are in bed would suit you, say so. Sometimes it can be helpful to talk away from your own home, in which case the social worker will be able to organise a meeting in his or her office. It's also worth making sure, while you're on the subject of visits, that you know how to get hold of the social worker, and also the team leader, in case you need someone in an emergency. You'll also need the number to ring if you have a crisis 'out of hours' between 5.30pm and 9am.

There will, of course, be times when the social worker simply can't avoid being late for or cancelling a visit, but you don't have to feel too sorry for this 'very busy' person. After all, full-time mothers and fathers are probably the busiest people around, and can't afford to waste time hanging about for visitors who don't turn up. (Having been both a social worker and a full-time mother of two young children, give me social work any day for a quiet life!) If necessary, make your feelings known on this subject!

The social worker has various purposes in mind when he or she visits a substitute family. Firstly, there is a legal, or statutory, aspect to the visit. Social workers have to check that the child is being properly looked after, physically and emotionally. In order to do this they need to see, occasionally, where the child sleeps, and to talk to you about all aspects of his or her life, such as school and health. Substitute parents can feel a bit put off by this part of the relationship with social workers, but if you remember that they are responsible for the child on behalf of the local authority or the parents, it's easier to accept this supervisory role as a part of the job.

Another important part of the social worker's job is seeing the child alone, so that there is an opportunity to talk about anything that might be bothering the child. Only very rarely are such meetings used to 'gripe' about

118

the foster or adoptive parents, but obviously if there are problems the child must be given the chance to air them. The social worker should always let you know the substance of these discussions, without breaking the child's confidence.

On every visit there will usually be plenty of information to exchange. The social worker will be telling you of any changes in the family circumstances or in the plans for the child. You will want to tell him or her about the child's progress at home and at school, and about visits from the family, if they take place at your home. It's very useful to keep a brief diary of events to jog your memory – after all, social workers have big thick files to remind them of what's happening in connection with a particular child, and would be appalled at the idea of having to remember intricate details of all the children they worked with. Indeed, dangerous mistakes could come from relying on memory. Traditionally, substitute parents haven't kept 'files' on the children they look after (obviously any written information would have to be kept very safely), but brief notes about significant events in the child's life with you could be invaluable.

You'll also want to use the social worker's visit as an opportunity to 'sound off' about any difficult behaviour or problems the child is causing, and hopefully you'll have confidence that the social worker will react to your concerns in a sympathetic but positive way. You need to feel that the person listening to your tale of woes really understands what you're saying, but isn't going to react too dramatically until he's sure this is warranted. Many substitute parents are reluctant to allow the social worker a view of the less than perfect side of the placement, in case his reaction to your irritation about Jimmy's dirty habits/ lying/stealing is to assume that you're asking for the child to be moved. However, you do have every right to talk freely about any aspects of the child that get on your nerves, and the social worker has a responsibility to listen without making snap judgements. You can help prevent

119

wires becoming crossed by making comments like 'Don't get me wrong, there's no way I want him to leave, but there are things about him that I find very trying; I wonder if you've got any ideas about how to handle them?'. Sometimes the social worker may have some ideas for changing the annoying behaviour, but sometimes he won't. You may just have to live with that particular behaviour for the time being and hope that the phase will pass. In the case of really distressing or dangerous behaviour, the social worker should be able to seek help from another professional, possibly a child psychiatrist. The important thing is for your response to the child to be taken seriously. It's been said earlier that behaviour that's tolerable for one person can be the last straw for another and lead to the early end of a placement. Make sure that your message, whatever it is, gets across!

At some point during the visit, the social worker should check with you that the purely practical side of the placement is satisfactory. Before the child moves in, foster parents are supplied with essentials such as cots, beds, chests of drawers, push chairs, and so on. Think hard about extra equipment that you might need for that particular child – a car seat, for example, or perhaps some cash towards the fitting of rear seat belts. Different departments will have different attitudes towards what's essential and what isn't, but unless you ask you won't find out what is available. Don't be shy. It could be helpful to put yourself in the social worker's place – would they struggle on without a desk or a telephone? Of course not! While the child is with you, things change – you may find that you need different equipment, and you should always let the social worker know what's required. This needn't necessarily be something just for the use of the foster child. If your washing machine breaks down it may be that you could be given help towards its repair. You'll never know till you ask, so don't suffer in silence!

Adoptive parents are usually treated rather differently from foster parents, in that it could be assumed that, if you had a child of your own, you would have had to find the money for extra equipment yourselves. However, if you're taking on a child with particular difficulties, two or three children at once, or are facing a situation where you will have to spend a lot of money quickly to enable you to look after the child properly, you must discuss this with the social worker to see if any help can be given.

Focusing on You

If you're in regular contact with a specialist social worker as well as the one attached to the child, or children, you're currently looking after, then your meetings with him or her will have a different focus. They will probably be far less frequent than your contacts with the child's social worker, and will be used to look at how you're managing as a substitute parent. Foster parents will be encouraged to review the previous placement and think about future children. For adopters, the contact with the home-finding social worker will probably be of most value in the waiting period before a child is placed, when reassurance that you haven't been forgotten and news of the children in need of homes is helpful.

As a foster parent your skills and experience grow with each placement, and it's important that your increasing value is fully recognised and used. After each placement has ended you should have the opportunity of looking back and listing what you did well and what you could have done better – and if you can feed a similar list back to the child's social worker to let him know what were his good and not so good points, so much the better! You may have surprised yourself by thoroughly enjoying the challenge of a teenage boy, although your original assessment stated that you prefer children under ten. You and the home-finding social worker need to discuss this, and if it seems that you might do well with another teenager your details must be altered to say that you've moved on from the type of child you first felt you could cope with.

These days social workers are realising that, whilst more new foster parents are always needed, it's equally important to find ways of keeping experienced foster parents who may tend to stop taking children if they don't feel properly used or valued. Training is important here, and good social services departments and child care organisations will arrange the occasional group meeting for approved foster parents to look at a particular topic in some depth. On the subject of training, many organisations, such as the National Foster Care Association and British Agencies for Adoption and Fostering, regularly organise training events that would be of great interest and value to many substitute parents. You might like to ask your department whether money is ever made available to pay for foster and adoptive parents to attend these sessions.

Many adoptive parents may find that they have little or no need of regular contact with a social worker once the placement is well under way, or certainly when the adoption order is finally made. However, you may find that you welcome the occasional visit or phone call from the social worker even after the making of the adoption order. Social workers and others used to believe that the day of the court hearing was also the day on which the family said goodbye to the social worker for ever. It was felt that if the family still needed contact with the social worker the time wasn't yet right for the adoption. However, it's now recognised that, whilst it can be right for the child and the family to go ahead with the adoption, that child's problems won't disappear magically with the granting of the order. So it can be helpful all round for the social worker to remain in touch, if only by saying 'I'm on the end of a phone if you need me'.

OTHER VISITORS

Depending on the child's age and whether or not he or she has any particular problems, you may have contact with a variety of other people during the placement, some as visitors and others whom you may see outside the home.

If you're looking after a baby or pre-school child, the health visitor will be an important and useful contact who can advise you on all the normal aspects of growing up, as she would any birth parent. She will also be able to check up on your foster or adoptive child's health records which will show general development as well as such things as whether he or she has had all the right vaccinations. You'll usually register the child with your own GP, unless you're fostering near enough to the birth parents' home to carry on with the original GP. When you first become a foster parent, it could be a good idea to tell your doctor that he or she can expect to see various children troop into the surgery with you over the next few years!

Substitute parents naturally have a good deal of contact with the schools that their charges attend, from an original registration right through to parents' evenings and the school play. It may be possible for the child to continue to attend the school he or she went to from home, and this is ideal if it can be arranged. If not, your own local school will probably accept children who are living with you. It's obviously important that the child's teachers have a good understanding of his or her circumstances, and any particular problems that might affect classwork and behaviour. However, it isn't always necessary for people such as teachers to know absolutely every detail of the child's history and the reasons for care. Before you make the first contact with the school you'll need to work out, probably with the social worker, what the staff need to know about the child, and what can be safely kept private. For example, there may be unhappy events in the child's history which he or she is very sensitive about, and which need not be revealed. Confidentiality is extremely important, and only those who really need it should have access to such information.

Children are always asked questions by their classmates when they go to a new school, and can be very embarrassed and upset by this if the truth is uncomfortable, and not something they want to talk about. Adults can sometimes help children work out a 'cover story' which can be truthful without being too revealing: 'I'm staying with friends/aunty and uncle/Pat and Dave at the moment because I can't live with Mum and Dad' might be enough to satisfy younger children, particularly if the foster child sounds happy and confident whilst giving this reply. A child placed permanently with a new family could say 'I've come to live with a new mum and dad because my first mum can't look after me'. Preparing the children for the fact that such questions will be asked is almost as important as planning what they should say.

If you're looking after a child with particular behaviour problems, or one who needs help to cope with a traumatic event such as sexual abuse, you may also have contact with a child psychologist, child psychiatrist or other therapist who specialises in work with children. Such a person will certainly be very interested in your observations of the child, but will also want to see him or her alone. This can mean that your living room is 'out of bounds' to the rest of the family for quite long periods, and it's important that you and the therapist make sure that the visits will take place at a convenient time for you and the family, as well as for the child.

Imagine yourself looking after a child who has regular contact in your home with his parents, and possibly with grandparents and brothers and sisters as well; his social worker visits once a fortnight and he's receiving extra help from a therapist on a weekly basis. This adds up to an awful lot of visitors in any one week, and could be typical of many placements. It's just another aspect of substitute care that needs careful thought before you embark on the process of becoming foster or adoptive parents.

Finally, think on this: 'Never be intimidated by professionals' should be sewn into a sampler to hang above the bed of every substitute parent! Every member of the child care team, including you, brings to each child's situation a particular level and quality of experience and skill. Your opinions are valuable and should be valued; the child will lose out in the end if you, his full-time carer, don't make sure that you say clearly what you think.

GETTING TOGETHER – LOCALLY AND NATIONALLY

Meeting with other substitute parents can be enjoyable and an important source of support before and after any children are placed with you. In many areas foster parents meet regularly for a variety of reasons. It's good to be able to share your particular problem of the moment with others who may have been there before you. Groups can organise discussions on different topics of interest, perhaps inviting a visiting speaker, and many local groups also arrange social and fund-raising events. Finally, a large number of foster parents with a common cause can act as a powerful pressure group in an attempt to alter departmental policy – a group of foster parents in a London borough successfully brought about a massive increase in allowances by threatening to refuse to accept any more children.

Many locally based groups of foster parents are affiliated to the National Foster Care Association. Membership of this large country-wide organisation, whose main aim is to promote the best possible practice in the field of substitute care, has many advantages for foster parents and it's possible to join individually as well as through your local group. Regular mailings keep members up to date not only with what's going on in the association but also in the whole field of child care, whilst the quarterly magazine is written primarily with foster parents in mind and carries articles on a range of topics. It can also be useful to know that there's always someone at the NFCA offices who will offer advice and help if you've got any sort of problem related to foster care, and they can often help sort out difficulties that may have arisen between you and the social services department. Most social services departments and child care organisations are corporate members of NFCA, and generally social workers in the field recognise the great value of this organisation, particularly to foster parents.

Adoptive parents don't have a national organisation on quite the same scale to call on, as the great majority of adopters settle into family life with their new children without needing, or wanting, to draw particular attention to their status by belonging to a group of other adoptive families. This is changing, however, and since adoptive families may continue to need support, this could come from other adopters as well as from a social worker. The Parent to Parent Information on Adoption Services is a national self-help group, established and run by adoptive parents, which aims to help those wanting to adopt to become matched with a child, and offers support, advice and encouragement to both prospective and existing adopters. This group is particularly keen to ensure that applicants are treated sympathetically by social services departments and other agencies, and if you feel that you have been treated badly as a prospective adopter in this respect, you may like to contact PPIAS for advice on where to turn for a more sensitive approach. This group publishes a newsletter three times a year, with many interesting articles, and also featuring a large number of children in need of new parents.

British Agencies for Adoption and Fostering is another national organisation which seeks to promote good standards of practice in the field of both fostering and adoption. The photo-listing service 'Be My Parent' (*see* Chapter 1), is run by BAAF, and is a very good method of ensuring that every child referred is made known to the widest possible range of families. Probably most people in the child care field would regard BAAF as more of a social workers' organisation, and the quarterly journal tends to feature weightier articles than those in either the NFCA or PPIAS publications. However, BAAF also publishes many books and booklets of great interest and value to prospective and existing substitute parents. The excellent *Adopting a Child*, for example, is a comprehensive guide to all the adoption agencies in the country, with indications of the types of children they are seeking to place, a general description of the adoption field, and what to expect when you're making an application. Again, BAAF staff would be happy to discuss problems or difficulties encountered by prospective adopters.

Finally, the Post-Adoption Centre is a unique organisation in that its staff become involved only *after* the adoption order has been made. They are available to work not only with adoptive parents and adopted children, but also with people whose own birth children have been adopted, and friends and relatives of any of these with queries or in need of advice. The centre also provides a service to those involved in a trans-racial adoption, and can help such families work out how to strengthen both family bonds and ethnic ties. It doesn't matter how long ago the adoption took place, the Post-Adoption Centre welcomes contact from anyone who may still, perhaps, be trying to come to terms with adoption after many years.

Full details about how to get in touch with all these organisations can be found at the back of the book.

6 The Legal Position

THE BACKGROUND

The law that relates to children in Britain is very complicated. It has been drawn up piecemeal over many decades,
so that there are dozens of different statutes and judgements which say what should happen to children who
can't live with their parents. At times, one piece of law
can appear to contradict another, and it takes a skilled
lawyer who is experienced in child care work to disentangle the threads. As foster or adoptive parents you
don't need to becomes familiar with all these complexities
– in fact most social workers have only a basic knowledge
of child care law – but it will be helpful for you to have
some idea of the legal position as it relates to you and to
any children you are looking after. You should always
discuss the child's legal position with the social worker,
and if you find yourself looking after a child who's in the
middle of an unusually complicated legal situation, you
may need to talk over your position with a solicitor as well.
New legislation is planned, which should make the law
somewhat easier to understand and to operate.

Don't feel surprised or annoyed when your social
worker admits that he or she doesn't have a full understanding of all the details of child care law. Many solicitors
struggle with it, and social workers simply do not have
time to familiarise themselves with all the details. You'll
probably find that the specialist home-finding social
worker is better informed on the law as it relates directly to
fostering and adoption than the child's social worker, as
they have a more limited area to deal with and can
therefore come to grips with it in greater depth.

If you need the services of a solicitor, try to make sure
that the firm you approach has someone who specialises in

child care law. The Law Society, which is the solicitors' governing body, now has a list of solicitors specially qualified to take on child care work, and you might like to consult this before making any contact with a particular practice. Social services departments, Citizens' Advice Bureaux and libraries should have copies. At the first meeting with your chosen solicitor, try to find out exactly what he or she is going to do on your behalf. Insist that explanations should be in language that you can understand! Solicitors have the reputation for being very expensive, and this could put you off consulting one, but you might find that you are eligible for legal aid, or that the child care agency which supervises your child may be prepared to help with costs.

THE LAW RELATING TO APPLICANTS

Social work practice in relation to people who want to become foster or adoptive parents is covered in Chapter 3. There are legal regulations that set out what duties the local authority or child care agency has in this area. The Boarding Out Regulations refer to fostering and the Adoption Agency Regulations to adoption, and both sets of regulations are fairly recent – the 1955 Boarding Out Regulations were redrafted in 1988, and are due to be published in the latter half of 1989, and the Adoption Agency Regulations came into force in 1984. Both are strictly legal documents and rather indigestible, but many professionals do refer to the notes which accompany and explain them, and which describe good practice. A Local Authority circular (LAC [84] 3) gives guidance on the Adoption Agency Regulations and the Boarding Out Guidance will have the same role with regard to the new Boarding Out Regulations.

For both fostering and adoption, the regulations make it clear what actions the social worker should take during the assessment to ensure that the applicants are suitable as substitute parents. The content of the social worker's report is covered, as are medicals and references. The composition of the Adoption or Fostering Panels who meet to consider whether or not an applicant is suitable is covered, along with the work of those groups. Specific statements are made about information that must be given, in writing, to the substitute parents, the birth parents and the child (if he or she is old enough to understand this) about what is happening. For example, everyone should be told in writing when the child went to live with the substitute family, and how long he or she is likely to stay there.

The Boarding Out Regulations look in detail at what happens after the placement has been made, for example, how often the social worker should visit. As a minimum, he or she must come to see the child and the new family within a week of the child moving in, every six weeks during the first year and every three months after that. The child's progress must be looked at in a review (a meeting involving those closely concerned with the child) within three months of placement, and then at least every six months. Foster parents themselves must be reviewed 'from time to time', and as a result of this they may continue to foster as before, perhaps move on to a different sort of fostering, or be told that they can't foster any more children. The written information given to foster parents at the time of approval should describe this review process, as well as the procedure for dealing with complaints by foster parents, arrangements made to cover any legal liabilities the foster parent may have as a result of the placement, and the arrangements for the child's financial support (how and when the allowances are paid).

These very new regulations go a long way towards giving foster parents more status as important members of the child care team, and in this way the law is catching up with good practice. Fostering is now recognised in law as a skilled task, rather than as an extension of mothering.

The Adoption Agencies Regulations also lay down stipulations about visits, reviews, and so on. The social worker must visit within a week of placement, as with fostering, but the timing of subsequent visits is left to the discretion of the adoption agency. The child's situation must be reviewed if the adopters haven't applied to the court for an adoption order after three months, although it is acknowledged that there will often be very good reasons why three months or even longer will elapse before the right time comes to make the application.

It's not necessary for you to have read the regulations, but it's useful for you to know that they exist, and that the social worker's contact with you has that legal framework.

THE LAW AND CHILDREN WHO NEED CARE

Voluntary or Statutory Care?

Children in care are there either because their parents have asked the social services for help, and have agreed that it would be best for the child to spend some time away from home, or because the social workers are so concerned about a child that they have asked the courts to agree to their removing that child against the parents' wishes.

If the parents are in agreement about their children being removed from home, those children are received into *voluntary care*. The word 'voluntary' simply explains that the child's parents *want* him or her to be in care, and they still have all their parental rights, and can ask for their children to be returned home at any time. They have every right to see their children while they are in care, although access will probably be restricted in some way for purely practical reasons. Social workers are not allowed to terminate access when children are in voluntary care. If you're fostering a child who's in care with the parents' agreement, you should talk to your social worker about what to do if the mother or father comes to your home

131

asking to take their child away. Parents have the right to resume care of their child, but the social worker would certainly want to know what was happening and to discuss the future with the parents before such action was taken. It's a fact that most children who come into voluntary care do go home within a short time. Whilst they are in care their parents should be helped to play a full part in discussions and plans for the future with the social worker, substitute parent and members of the child care team.

The other way into care is through a decision of the court (usually the juvenile court), and this is often called *statutory care*. In these cases the parents usually don't want their children to be removed from home, and social workers have to ask the court for an order allowing them to take the child away against the parents' wishes. Obviously this can't be done without good reason, and the court will hear evidence about the child and family which will try to show that the child is not being properly looked after. Children who are being physically hurt or sexually abused can be taken from their parents in this emergency fashion.

Care Orders

A court order enabling a child to be removed from home in an emergency can only last for a very short time, and then the juvenile court will meet to hear a great deal of information about the child's situation, in order to help it come to the best decision about that child's future. The social worker will relate the family circumstances as he or she found them, and there may also be evidence from a health visitor, teacher, doctor or specialist called in to give an expert opinion on one particular aspect of the case. All these people will be questioned by the solicitor for the local authority, the parents' solicitor, and the solicitor who represents the child. The parents can give evidence, as can other people whose evidence may support their case, and it *is* possible for the child to talk to the court directly, although this doesn't happen very often. Also involved will be an independent social worker called a *guardian ad litem*. This person is appointed by the court to look at the whole situation with a fresh eye, and to tell the court what she or he thinks would be the best outcome for the child. The guardian will need to see the child many times, since an important part of the job is finding out what the child thinks about what's already happened and what should happen in the future. If you're fostering a child whose case is about to be considered by the juvenile court, you'll almost certainly be visited by that child's *guardian ad litem*, as he or she will want to talk to you about the child and will be interested in your views.

It is possible that the child's foster parents may themselves be asked to give evidence in court, if they have some particular information about the child that would be useful for the court to hear. Most people (including social workers!) are anxious about court appearances, if not downright scared stiff. If you were to be called upon to give evidence you should have the opportunity to discuss the questions you'll be asked very thoroughly with the social worker, and also with the local authority solicitor, so that you'll know what to expect. (The NFCA publishes a very useful leaflet on this subject called *Coping with court – a guide for foster parents*.)

If the juvenile court decides that the child cannot be looked after by his or her parents because they are not able to provide the right sort of care, it will make the child the subject of a *care order* (new legislation may soon change the name to 'parental rights order' or something similar). In this situation, the social services department will take over the parental rights for that child. This means that social workers will make all the decisions about the child that are usually made by parents, such as where he or she lives and goes to school. The parents still have a very important part to play in their children's lives, however, and social workers should talk to them very fully about any decisions that are being considered, and take account of their opinions and what they would like to happen to the child. Children themselves also have opinions, wishes and feelings about their circumstances, and social workers should make sure that they listen closely to these as well.

Wardship

You may find yourself fostering a child who is a *ward of court.* This means that someone with an interest in the child's well-being (this could be a relative such as a grandparent or the father of an illegitimate child, a foster parent or the local authority) has put the child's situation before the High Court, and has asked that court to reach a decision about what's best for the child. As soon as the application for wardship has been made, the child's position becomes 'frozen'. No one can move the child or make any important decisions about his or her life without the court's permission.

Wardship is used by the local authority when it seems that the powers of the juvenile court are not sufficient to sort out a complicated situation. Relatives other than parents don't usually have the right to make their views known to the juvenile court, or to start proceedings in that court, so they may use wardship as a way of gaining some control over the child's situation. The court which deals with wardship is very much more flexible than the juvenile court, and can make a variety of different decisions about the child. As foster or adoptive parents you could be made parties in wardship proceedings. In other words, you would have the right to be represented in court (usually by a solicitor) and to make your views known. You could also initiate wardship proceedings yourself, if for some reason you felt that the child's position was so unsatisfactory that the High Court should be asked to sort it out. Initiating wardship proceedings is a very serious and possibly costly step, however, and if you are involved in any way in wardship it's essential to seek the advice of a solicitor who is experienced in this type of work.

134

Access

The question of contact between the child in care and his or her own family has been dealt with in some detail in Chapter 4. Laws came into operation in 1984 which tell social workers how access should be handled, and in particular what to do if it is decided that the parents should no longer see the child – that access should be terminated.

Termination of access is a very serious step. It should only be considered when contact with the parents seems to be causing the child great distress (perhaps he is really afraid that his mum or dad will harm him), or when it has become obvious to the social workers that this child isn't going to be able to live with his natural parents again, and further contact with them will not benefit the child at all. In this situation, the social workers have a duty to inform the parents of their decision, and to make it clear to them how they can say what they think. The parents' own social worker should then personally give them the legal notice which terminates access to their child.

If the birth parents still disagree with the decision, they can apply to the juvenile court for an *access order*. The court would hear evidence from the social workers and the parents (and in some circumstances foster parents can also make their views known to the court), and a *guardian ad litem* would be appointed, as in care proceedings (*see* page 133). The court must decide whether it was right for the social workers to terminate access or not. If it disagrees with the social workers' decision it can make an *access order* which gives the natural parents the legal right to see their child.

Sometimes social workers want to restrict access without actually stopping it altogether. They are allowed to do this under the law, but it must not be used as a way round the access legislation. In other words, it would be quite wrong to let a parent see his or her child only two or three times a year, unless the parent and child were in agreement with

135

this, as this sort of contact would quickly become meaningless for the child. Because the social workers had not actually terminated access, the parent could not complain to the juvenile court, so they would have no means of trying to get the decision changed. Many people think that parents should have the right to ask the court to look at the issue of access even when it has not been terminated, but at present the law does not allow this.

CUSTODIANSHIP

The law sets out who can apply for a custodianship order, and whether or not the agreement of the child's parents or the social services department is needed.

A relative (grandparent, aunt, uncle, brother or sister), or in some circumstances a stepparent, can apply to be custodian of a child, as long as that child has been living with him, her or them for three months before the application is made. They would need the consent of the child's parent, or, if the child is in care, the local authority. Anybody, including a foster parent, can apply for custodianship if they have been looking after a child for twelve months (this doesn't have to be a continuous period, but must include the three months immediately before the application). Again, they would need to get the consent of the parents or local authority.

When a child has been living with the people who want to become custodians for three years (not necessarily continuous, but including the three months prior to the application), they do not have to have the consent of the person who has legal custody of the child (the parents or local authority).

The person, or people (you can be a custodian either as a single person or jointly with another person) who want to become custodians have to apply either to the magistrates' court or the county court, and they have to tell the local authority in whose area they live what they have done. The local authority will be a party to the proceedings, which means the court will hear the social workers' opinion on whether a custodianship order is best for the child. The social worker will also write a report, giving details of the applicants and the child, and assessing the relationship between them. The child's parents will also be party to the proceedings, so the court will hear their views too. The social worker's report will contain details of the birth parents, their relationship with the child, and whether it is likely that they will be able to care for their child in the future. If the child is in voluntary care, and consent is needed, the parents will be asked to give this. If the child is in statutory care, the local authority, which has parental rights over the child, has to give consent. Whatever the situation with regard to consent, the parents should always be fully consulted by the social workers about what's happening to their child.

Foster parents who decide that they want to become custodians of a foster child will, no doubt, discuss this very thoroughly with the social worker, and in most cases the application will be made with the agreement of the local authority. You don't have to have the backing of the social workers, unless of course you actually need their legal consent to the application. There will be some cases in which foster parents will apply without the local authority's support, and they are perfectly entitled to do so. However, bearing in mind that the court will take into account the social workers' views, it's obviously better if everyone is in agreement. If you feel strongly that custodianship is right for the child, no matter what the social workers say, you should certainly get legal advice from a solicitor. The court makes the final decision, and has as its prime consideration what's best for the child, not the applicants.

If a custodianship order is made, it will last until the child is eighteen, unless revoked by the court. If the situation changes, the custodians, the local authority, or the parents can ask the court to revoke the order. As with the original application, the court will listen to everyone's views and then make its decision based on what is thought to be best for the child. If it does decide that the child should no longer be subject to a custodianship order, then that child will become again the responsibility of the parents, if that was the case before the order was made, or the local authority if he or she was in care before the making of the original order. If the court is not happy about the child going back to the parents it can make a care order.

For more details on the question of access to children on custodianship orders *see* Chapter 2. Briefly, the court can order that contact with a child's family should continue, and the custodians must comply with this. If anyone involved isn't happy about access, the court which made the order can be asked to consider again whether it's right for the child to go on seeing his or her natural family.

Custodians have most of the rights and duties that parents have, including deciding where the child should go to school and so on. They *can't* agree to the adoption of the child, or to his or her emigration. The child does not take on the custodians' name – it's important to remember this, as many fostered children do take their foster parents' surname on an informal basis. The law on custodianship makes it clear that no change of name should be made without consulting the birth parents and possibly the court as well. Custodians should bring the child up in his or her religion, according to the wishes of the parents, if this is at all possible.

ADOPTION

Parental Agreement

Perhaps the most important legal point about adoption is the fact that the parents' agreement must be sought in all cases, no matter who the applicants are or how long the child has been living with them. The only exception to this relates to the child's father if he was not married to the mother. He is known in law as the 'putative father', and does not have to give his consent to adoption, although he should always be consulted about plans for his child if at all possible.

When an adoption order is made, the ties between the child and his or her birth parents are severed completely, and the order cannot be revoked, so obviously it is crucial that the parents are fully aware of what's happening and are able to say what they think. In many situations the parents will probably have talked at length with the social worker about what's best for their child and will be in agreement with the adoption. There are some cases where the parent does not want his or her child to be adopted, and in these cases the applicants must ask the court (magistrates' or county) to 'dispense with agreement'. This means that the adoption order is made even though the child's parents do not want this to happen. Before the court can decide to do this, it has to consider very carefully whether the parents' agreement should indeed be over-ridden, and the law lays down six different ways in which this can happen. These grounds, as they are called, are all to do with the parents failing in some way to provide adequate care for the child, either because they have not looked after the child properly in the past, have ill-treated the child, have abandoned or neglected the child, or are being 'unreasonable' in not agreeing to the adoption. The court can also dispense with a parent's agreement if it can be proved that he or she cannot be found.

If you are applying to adopt a child whose parents are not in agreement with the adoption, you will certainly need the help of a solicitor. Depending on your income, you may be eligible for legal aid to help pay the costs of your application, or the social services department or child care agency may have a policy of meeting the legal expenses of a contested adoption. You certainly shouldn't worry too much about legal costs, as it's very unlikely that you would be paying them personally.

The social worker should have put you in the picture as far as the child's background is concerned, and he or she will probably discuss with your solicitor how to go about asking the court to make the order without parental agreement. Such situtations are worrying for the would-be adoptive parents, who dread the day of the court hearing in case the court does not think it right to overrule the parents' wishes. It's worth remembering two things if you find yourself in this position. Firstly, the social worker wouldn't have recommended adoption for this child in the first place if he or she, along with the other members of the child care team, had not thought it likely that the court case would be successful. Secondly, if the court did decide that it was not right to sever all contact with the parents and make the adoption order, this won't necessarily result in the child being removed from your care. The social workers would want to consider anew the plans for the child, but could well conclude that he or she should remain with you as a foster child, particularly if you've been looking after him or her for some time.

When the parents are not in agreement with the adoption, the court will appoint a *guardian ad litem*, as for care proceedings, who will look at the whole situation, ensure that everything has been done properly, and verify that the child's and the parents' views have been fully taken into account. This person will also write a report for the court. When the case comes to court for the final hearing (there may have been one or more short hearings before the court is ready to consider all the evidence), your solicitor will make sure the judge or the magistrates hear evidence supporting the fact that you want to adopt the child. The parents' solicitor will tell the court, with the help of witnesses, the reasons why the parents' agreement should not be dispensed with. Since in many cases the child's birth parents and the adoptive parents have not met, and it's not thought right that they should meet, it's usually possible for the adoptive parents to wait elsewhere in the court building while the first part of the hearing is taking place. If the court decides that the birth parents' wishes should be overruled and their agreement dispensed with, the adoptive parents and the child will then go into court so that the judge or magistrates can see them before making their final decision.

If the parents are in agreement with the making of an adoption order, the court still appoints an independent social worker, called a *reporting officer*. This person will talk to the birth parent or parents, make sure that they understand exactly what it is they are agreeing to, and witness their signature(s) on the form agreeing to the adoption.

The court has to make two separate decisions in an adoption hearing. Firstly, it must decide whether the parents agree to the adoption or whether it should go ahead without their agreement, and secondly, it must decide whether the applicants are right for the child. When the court is happy about both these aspects, the adoption order can be made.

Sometimes the court is asked to look at the first matter, to do with the parents' agreement, without at the same time deciding whether a specific person or couple should adopt that child. This procedure is called *freeing for adoption*. If you have a child placed with you who has already been freed, you will know that you don't have to worry about whether the parents are in agreement or not, since the court has already made its decision on that issue. It's possible to place a child with prospective adopters and then ask the court to free him or her before the couple actually apply to adopt. This could happen in a situation where the social workers knew that the parents were against the idea of adoption, and wanted to protect the adoptive family from being involved in a distressing battle in court. When the application to adopt a child who is already freed is heard by the court, it simply has to decide the question of whether the applicants and child are right for each other.

Unless you are related to the child (grandparent, uncle, aunt, brother or sister), you can only apply to adopt a child who has been placed with you by a recognised adoption agency, such as a local authority or other child care organisation. This law was introduced to put an end to so-called 'third party' adoptions, for example, when a mother who couldn't look after her baby simply asked a friend to adopt the child. These situations weren't subject to any checks by social workers, and sometimes ended unhappily.

When the court considers an adoption application, it will have before it a report written by the social worker which includes information about the child, birth family and adoptive family. The law states exactly what this report should contain, and much of its content will be similar to the information in the original assessment report on prospective adopters.

This isn't a legal text book, and the information given in this chapter represents only the briefest look at some parts of the law that might affect you in your role as foster or adoptive parents. Every child's position with regard to the law will be different, and you should always make sure that you know what sort of order that child is on, who has parental rights, who has the right to sign consent for medical treatment, and so on. All this information will normally form part of the written agreement you enter into with the social workers at the beginning of every placement. If not, you must ask for a written explanation of the child's legal position.

In other words, don't look to this chapter for detailed legal information to help you understand precisely your child's position, because it's unlikely that you will find it. The information given here is very general, and you will need to rely on the social worker and possibly a solicitor for a specific interpretation of the child's situation.

Conclusion

The perfect family doesn't exist, nor does the perfect mother or father. As parents, we all have different ideas about what's right for our children, and it's up to us to work out the best way of bringing them up and preparing them for adulthood. Every family has its problems and every parent has times when his or her patience simply runs out. In most families children survive these difficult times unharmed, but some parents do become overwhelmed by their problems. In this situation, the state has to become involved to ensure the safety and well-being of the children. All children, whatever their colour or culture, have certain basic needs that must be met, and substitute parents can provide for these when the birth parents, for whatever reason, can't manage to give their children the love and care they need.

The job we do as parents, whether birth, foster or adoptive, is daunting in its emotional and physical demands, and in its importance, not only to the children we look after but to society as a whole. In a few years' time that society will be made up of adults who have been moulded by our care. If you have read this far, you're presumably still interested in looking after other people's children and haven't been too alarmed by the many possible pitfalls and problems that I have outlined. My intention has been to put you off only if you don't really want to become a substitute parent. My experience is that those of you who are one hundred per cent committed to the idea will probably have become even more determined to succeed as you have read the preceding chapters.

I have met dozens of foster and adoptive parents during my career in social work, and generally I have found them to be happy, friendly people with confidence in themselves and in what they are doing. The foster parents love children (this doesn't mean that they fall in love with every child they look after), enjoy their company, and are honest enough to say 'That could have been me' when they hear about parents who simply haven't been able to deal with their own difficulties and give their children the right sort of care. The adopters want to fall in love with a particular child, and have many of the same qualities as foster parents. However, they are very different beings in terms of what they want out of substitute parenting. They'll put up with the social workers, the medicals, the whole business of assessment and introduction to a child, but they look forward to the time when they can settle down to family life without the toing-and-froing of social workers, parents and children which is meat and drink to foster parents.

I hope this book has helped you distinguish between the two forms of substitute care, and let you make up your mind which is for you. I hope it's given you an idea what it's all about, and what you can expect, both before and after the child comes to stay with you. Above all, I hope it's given you a sense of the value of substitute parents. They haven't been properly valued in the past, and it's now up to the social workers and the substitute parents themselves to make sure that they are seen as vital people in the network of those who provide care for children and plan for their future. To do this successfully, foster and adoptive parents need good support and training, and foster parents (and in some cases adopters) should get proper pay for a proper job – if you do go on to become substitute parents, fight for these as your rights!

Finally, we musn't forget the voice of the consumer – after all, the child is the most important person and the focus of attention of the child care team. I thought I would end the book with some comments from children on living with other people's mums and dads.

'Kath and Steve [foster parents] are really nice and I like it here. There are plates and saucepans here, and the pop man comes. We go out to good places. But I still love my mum and I want to go home.'

(Eight-year-old boy who had lived in squalid conditions with a mum who loved him but couldn't cope. The plan is for him to go home when her skills improve.)

'It's good here, in my foster home, but I want to go home. The nice thing is that mum comes every day and she has her tea with us.'

(Nine-year-old sister of the boy above.)

'I didn't like living with my mum and her boyfriend because I was burnt and hit. I want to live with my new mum [foster mother] and I don't want her [birth mother] to visit.'

(Four-year-old boy fostered after having been physically abused by both mother and partner. This little lad was able to be very clear about what he wanted to happen.)

'I had a first mum and I know why she couldn't look after me. It makes me sad when I look at this [life story book] but I know I've got my new mum and dad for good.'

(Eight-year-old girl placed for adoption.)

'It will be good when I am adopted. I will feel so different and the social worker won't have to keep visiting – that makes me feel very different.'

(Eleven-year-old girl awaiting the adoption hearing.)

'Now I'm here [foster home], I know what's going to happen each day.'

(Six-year-old girl, fostered following non-accidental injury.)

'I feel safe here.'

(Five-year-old boy removed from home and fostered because there was a high risk that he would be injured.)

Glossary

Every profession has its own jargon, and social work is no exception. Social workers should try not to use words that are not understood by everyone, but there are a few words that are so commonly used by people who work with children in care that I have listed them with their meanings. Also included are some legal words and phrases that are frequently used by solicitors and social workers working with children who are before the courts.

Abuse   Harm caused to a child by an adult, either physical, involving actual injury, sexual, which may involve physical injury and will certainly leave psychological scars or emotional, involving neglect. Physical abuse is sometimes referred to as 'non-accidental injury.'

Access   Contact between children in care and their parents or other members of their families. This usually means meetings, but can refer to other sorts of contact such as letters and telephone calls. In exceptional cases, the local authority can decide to terminate, or stop, access.

Adoption   The means by which a child becomes a full member of a new family. When a court makes an adoption order, it is, legally, as if that child had been born to the adoptive parents.

Attachment   The special ties of affection that grow between a child and the adults who look after him, usually his parents.

Birth Parent   The biological mother or father of the child, often called 'natural parent'. The father of an illegitimate child (a child born to parents who are not married) is not, in law, a parent; this means he does not have to give his agreement to adoption, and he may not have the same rights as the mother in other court proceedings.

Care The blanket term used to cover the status of children who cannot live with their own parents, and who are looked after by the state, usually in foster homes or children's homes. A child in 'voluntary care' is there with the parents' agreement, whereas a child in 'statutory care', usually on a care order, has often been brought before the juvenile court because of some problem at home, and is probably in care against the parents' wishes.

Care Order If the court makes a care order in respect of a child, all the decisions about the child are made by the social workers. The parents are consulted, and if they are very unhappy about the situation or feel that they should be able to look after their child themselves, they can ask the court to revoke the care order. Sometimes children on care orders can live at home with their parents, but this would be closely supervised by the social workers, who would still be responsible for the important decisions about the child. Unless it is revoked the care order lasts until the child is eighteen.

Child Care Agency This phrase has been used to indicate organisations other than local authority social services departments who are involved with children who can't live with their own families – for example, Barnardo's, Children's Society.

Child Care Team This phrase has been used throughout the book to refer to the group of people who, together, make plans and decisions about a child in care. This group will include the social worker, the foster parents or children's home staff, the birth parent(s), other professionals such as health visitor or teacher, and the child if he or she is old enough to join in some of the discussions, certainly with the social worker if not with the whole group.

Children's Homes Can be run either by the local authority or other child care agencies, to look after children in care for whom living with a substitute family either is not possible, or is not thought to be best for the child. Usually cater for teenagers rather than younger children.

147

Custodianship A half-way status between fostering and adoption, which allows the custodians to make most of the important decisions about the child. Lasts until the child is eighteen unless revoked.

Disruption The ending of a placement, either foster or adoptive, before it is planned that it should end. Often called 'breakdown'.

Fostering When a child in care is looked after by approved foster parents, on behalf of the local authority social services department or other child care agency. Foster parents should always be involved in planning for the child, but can't take any important decisions about the child without consulting the social workers and/or the birth parents.

Guardian ad Litem An independent social worker who can be appointed by the court to look at all the circumstances surrounding the child and the court hearing. This person will not be part of the local authority which has responsibility for the child, hence their independence.

Local Authority The umbrella organisation which includes the social services department, housing, education, and so on, in any one county or metropolitan borough. When a child is in care the local authority is the body with legal responsibility for the child, and this is then delegated to the social services department.

Placement The word used to describe the child living with a foster or adoptive family: 'Jimmy was placed on such-and-such a date, and the placement is going well.'

Putative Father The legal term for the child's father, when he was not married to the child's mother at the time of birth.

Rehabilitation The child returning home to live with the birth parent(s). As in 'The plan for Wayne is rehabilitation'.

Reporting Officer An independent social worker appointed by the court in adoption proceedings when the parent(s) are in agreement with the adoption. The reporting officer will visit the parents and witness their signatures giving formal agreement.

Review   A meeting of a group of people closely involved with a child in care to consider his or her progress during the last six months (or shorter period), and to plan for the future. Foster parents and adopters can also be reviewed. The social worker and substitute parent will talk together about recent placements and plan the best way of using the family in the future.

Revocation   If a care order or custodianship order is revoked, this means that the court agrees to cancel it so that the child's status goes back to what it was before the order was made.

Sibling   Brother or sister. 'Sibling group' is often used to describe two or more brothers and sisters who need to be together in a new family.

Social Services Department   The section of the local authority which deals not only with children, but also with anybody in need of help such as the elderly, physically and mentally handicapped, and mentally ill.

Social Worker   Works for either the social services department or other child care agency. May specialise in child care work or fostering and adoption, or could work with the whole range of people who need help.

Substitute Parent/Family   Collective term for foster or adoptive parents. They are looking after the child as substitutes for the child's birth parents.

Further Reading

Listed below are some of the many books and leaflets published on the topics of fostering and adoption. Many are published by either British Agencies for Adoption and Fostering (BAAF) or the National Foster Care Association (NFCA), and can be obtained by post from these organisations. A complete list of their publications will be sent on request. Other publications may be ordered through your local bookshop.

BOOKS

About You and Fostering (NFCA)
Workbook for teenagers moving from residential care to foster care; attractively produced, could be used by foster parents or social workers.

Adopting a Child: A Guide for People Interested in Adoption (BAAF)
Invaluable for would-be adopters; gives information on the process, and addresses of all adoption agencies.

Adoption, the Inside Story, Austin, J. (Barn Owl Books)
Written by adoptive parents – real life stories.

Against the Odds – Adopting Mentally Handicapped Children, Macaskill, C. (BAAF)
A study of 20 families who adopted such children.

Everything You Need to Know about Adoption, Jones, M. (Sheldon House)
Excellent guide, including useful information on inter-country adoption.

Explaining Adoption, Chennells, P. (BAAF)
Very helpful guide on how to handle this sensitive area.

For Ever and Ever – Adopting an Older Child, Jewett, C. (BAAF)
Covers the whole process of adopting an older child, and includes personal accounts of adoption.

Fostering in the Eighties, Rowe, J. (BAAF)
Overview of the current fostering scene, looking at the tasks today's foster parents are asked to undertake.

Fostering – the Hidden Feelings, (Northern Ireland FCA)
Articles written by foster parents, foster children, parents of children in care, relatives and neighbours on how family life changes when you become a foster family. Very useful for those thinking about fostering.

House of Tomorrow, Lorrimer, C. (Corgi)
The true story of an extraordinary foster mother, Jeanette Roberts, herself deprived and abused as a child, who has fostered or adopted thirty children, many with backgrounds similar to her own.

Life Books for Children in Care, (Northern Ireland FCA)
Encourages the use of life books, emphasises the need for a sensitive approach, and gives concrete examples of how this has been done in a variety of settings by different people.

Making Life Story Books, Ryan, T. and Walker, R. (BAAF)
Practical guide on how to help children make these books – well illustrated, with examples of different approaches and techniques.

Rewards in Foster Care, (Northern Ireland FCA)
Foster parents and children write about how they grew through foster care.

Room for One More, Miller, B. (NFCA)
Highly recommended for would-be foster parents, this is a very funny, and readable, account of life as a foster mum.

Leaflets

The National Foster Care Association publishes many very useful and interesting leaflets, aimed mainly at practising foster parents, but several would be of interest to prospective foster parents. For a full list, write to or phone NFCA at Francis House, Francis Street, London SW1P 1DE, 01 828 6266.

British Agencies for Adoption and Fostering also publishes several useful leaflets, again of interest to prospective foster parents and also to prospective adopters. For a full list, write or phone BAAF at 11 Southwark Street, London SE1 1RQ, 01 407 8800.

BOOKS FOR CHILDREN

Several books have been written specifically for children in adoptive or foster homes; the following are a few examples.

Bruce's Story, Thom, M. and Macliver, C. (Children's Society)
(Available through either BAAF or NFCA)
Bruce, a 'spaniel sort of dog', tells how he had to leave his mum and dad and how he came eventually to live with a new family. Young children will enjoy the story and can identify with Bruce.

Jane is Adopted, Althea (Souvenir Press)
A simple story book for children up to about seven or eight.

Jenny and the Cat Club, Averill, E. (Collins)
A stray cat who is 'adopted' has to learn to fit in to her new surroundings. When her master adopts two brothers, life becomes more difficult for Jenny, but it all works out in the end.

Joey, van der Meer, Ron and Atie (NFCA)
Picture storybook about how Joey copes with his short-term foster home. Honest and imaginative, with full colour illustrations.

I am Adopted, Lapsley, S. (The Bodley Head)
Beautifully illustrated story for young children – Charles and Sophie are adopted, and Charles says that 'adoption means belonging'.

Find a Stranger, Say Goodbye, Lowry, L. (Viking Kestrel)
This is more suitable for older children, and is a story about an adopted girl and her search for her birth mother. When she finds her, she also discovers that her adopted parents are her 'real' family, and returns to live with them.

Useful Addresses

British Agencies for Adoption and Fostering
11 Southwark Street
London SE1 1RQ
01 407 8800

A registered charity and professional organisation for all those working in the child care field. Will give advice on adoption and fostering to members of the public; helps put children in need of new families in touch with those families. Membership open to anyone with an interest in this field, including adoptive parents.

Family Rights Group
6–9 Manor Gardens
Holloway Road
London N7 6LA
01 263 4016/9724

A group of social workers, lawyers, and other people (could include substitute parents) who want to improve the law and practice relating to children in care, and to families in contact with statutory agencies.

The National Association for the Childless
318 Summer Lane
Birmingham B19 3RL
021 359 4887

A self-help organisation for people with fertility problems, offering advice and counselling. Quarterly newsletter.

The National Foster Care Association
Francis House
Francis Street
London SW1P 1DE
01 828 6266

Offers membership to foster parents, social workers and others concerned about the quality of care for children. Can advise on issues connected with fostering. Concerns itself with finding homes/families for children.

The National Organisation for Counselling
Adoptees and their Parents
3 New High Street
Headington
Oxford OX3 7AJ
0865 750554

A support group of adopters and adopted people, which can put you in touch with people who have had similar experiences. This could be helpful if your adopted child decides he or she wants to contact his or her birth family, and you would like the opportunity of discussing your worries about this.

Parent to Parent Information on Adoption Services
Lower Boddington
Daventry
Northamptonshire NN11 6YB
0327 60295

Aims to help potential adopters by passing on information about how and where to apply, and to provide support, advice and encouragement for prospective and existing adopters, and long-term foster parents. Puts adoptive families in touch with one another so that they can share their joys and their difficulties. Helps ensure that families and children are 'matched' by promoting children's needs through the newsletter.

Post-Adoption Centre
Gregory House
48 Mecklenburgh Square
London WC1N 2NU
01 833 3214/5

A professional service which deals exclusively with the unique issues which may arise after an adoption. Provides counselling for adopted people, adoptive families and birth parents whose child was adopted – open to anyone, free of charge, who has been involved in an adoption.

Index